Behavioral Objectives

A GUIDE TO INDIVIDUALIZING LEARNING

Language Arts

JOHN C. FLANAGAN
ROBERT F. MAGER
WILLIAM M. SHANNER

Westinghouse Learning Press
Palo Alto, California

Division of Westinghouse Learning Corporation

Library of Congress Catalog Card Number: 79–149051

First Edition

Printed in the United States of America

CONTENTS

CONTENTS

Preface

A huge advantage of an instructional objective derives from the simple fact that it is written. Once it is written, it is visible. Once it is visible, it can be reviewed, evaluated, modified, and improved.

Objectives are frequently discussed but seldom seen. In these volumes you can see approximately four thousand instructional objectives in the subject areas of language arts, mathematics, science, and social studies ranging from grade one through grade twelve. This collection represents the cooperative efforts of over one hundred classroom teachers and an almost equal number of staff members at the American Institute for Research and Westinghouse Learning Corporation.

Since these volumes present written objectives rather than a discussion about objectives, they become the criteria by which materials are selected, content outlined, instructional procedures and educational technology developed, and tests and examinations prepared. All these aspects of an educational program are really the means for accomplishing the basic educational purpose.

This collection serves to stimulate teachers and educators in selecting and developing behavioral objectives for their own use. These objectives may be criticized and evaluated, revised and modified; objectives may be added or deleted, all with the purpose of arriving at an appropriate set of educational outcomes to meet the educational needs of a local situation and of individual students.

The rather obvious purpose of an instructional objective should be to make clear to teachers, students, and other interested persons what youngsters should be able to do as a result of the instructional program. A well-written instructional objective should specify under what conditions and to what extent a certain kind of student performance can be expected.

Unfortunately, school systems commonly lack a comprehensive and reasonably consistent set of educational objectives. Educational goals and objectives are frequently expressed only in broad, global terms, and the question of what and how to teach is left to a considerable extent to the teacher. As a result, quality in the

PREFACE

schools is closely associated with the qualified and skillful teacher. No doubt considerable excellent educational work is done by artistic teachers who, while they may not have a clear conception of goals, do have an intuitive sense of good teaching. Their materials are significant, and they develop topics effectively with students. They clarify the educational objectives (even objectives not directly stated) through their actions as they teach intuitively.

If the foregoing were to serve as a basis for defining education, then the "intuitiveness of the artistic teacher" would have to be built into the educational program. This, of course, cannot be done. The alternative is to start with clearly defined, rather than implied, instructional objectives.

Educational objectives—even clearly stated, specific objectives —are, in the final analysis, matters of choice and thus are value judgments. The question then arises:

> Who provides these value judgments? In the last analysis, the public schools are operated to meet the needs of society. Some of the objectives, along with rules regarding who shall attend school, are provided for in state constitutions and by-laws. Other objectives are set forth by the efforts of elected representatives of the people of a community. Some are provided by professional educators hired to operate the schools. Still others come from our knowledge of children themselves and how they learn. All of these sources effectively furnish the educational objectives for a local public school. Objectives will change with the changing conditions of the times, sometimes quickly, as with Sputnik, but usually slowly.

In evaluating and summarizing instructional objectives, whatever their source, certain kinds of information and knowledge provide a more intelligent basis than others for making decisions about objectives. If certain facts are known and understood, the probability is increased that judgments about objectives will be wise and that educational goals will gain in significance, objectivity, and validity. For this reason the so-called scientific study of the curriculum has largely concerned itself with investigations that may provide a more adequate basis for wise selection of instructional objectives than has previously been available.

What sources can be used for acquiring information from which objectives can be derived? This question has been the subject of much controversy between essentialists and progressives, between

PREFACE

subject specialists and child psychologists, between sociologists and philosophers, between this school group and that school group.

Progressives and child psychologists emphasize the importance of studying the child to find out what kinds of interests he has, what problems he encounters, what purposes he has in mind. They see this information as providing the basic source for selecting objectives. Essentialists and subject specialists, on the other hand, are impressed by the large body of knowledge collected over many thousands of years, the so-called cultural heritage, and emphasize this body of knowledge as the primary source for deriving objectives. They view objectives as essentially the basic learnings selected from the vast cultural heritage of the past.

Many sociologists and others concerned with the pressing problems of contemporary society see in an analysis of today's world the basic information from which objectives can be derived. They view the school as the agency for helping young people to deal effectively with the critical problems of life in modern society. If existing problems can be determined, then, the sociologist feels, the objectives of the school are to provide the knowledge, skills, and attitudes that will help people to deal intelligently and effectively with contemporary problems. On the other hand, educational philosophers recognize that there are basic values in life, largely transmitted from one generation to another by means of education. They see the school as aiming essentially at the transmission of basic values derived by comprehensive philosophic study; hence they view educational philosophy as the source from which objectives can be derived.

The point of view recommended here is that no single source of information is adequate as a basis for wise and comprehensive decisions about the objectives of education. Each of the sources described has certain values to commend it. Each source should be given consideration in planning. In this way educational programs may be developed that are flexible and suitable for any specific public-school situation, regardless of whether that situation is influenced primarily by a single viewpoint or by a combination of attitudes concerning educational objectives.

Although the objectives in these volumes contribute to solving the difficult problem of delineating a curriculum, they should not be considered as a final and perfect product. Any set of objectives must in fact be considered tentative, requiring continuous updating

PREFACE

and reevaluation to the educational purposes and programs at hand. To have critical comments made about one's objectives should be taken as a compliment, since criticism can only be made when one has given the thought and taken the time to write the objectives down.

In spite of the great effort and the number of man-hours that have gone into the task of compiling the objectives in these volumes, several of the objectives listed cannot yet be considered to be "true objectives," if by objectives we mean instructional outcomes described in terms of performance. In fact, the editors wish to make the following comments as to why some of the objectives herein are open to multiple interpretation.

1. Some objectives describe a classroom activity taking place during the process of learning, rather than the performance to be exhibited by the proficient student after learning.

2. Some objectives lack a description of, or even a suggestion for, the stimulus conditions under which a student is to perform. Conversely (and perversely), seemingly unimportant stimulus conditions are occasionally included.

3. Some statements (this term seems more appropriate here than objectives) fail to suggest any sort of criteria. Though not all objectives demand criteria, this lack makes for a certain vagueness in the phrasing of some objectives.

With slight editorial and organizational modifications, the objectives in these volumes are the objectives for Project PLAN. Project PLAN is a system of individualized education, operative at grades one through twelve in the subject areas of language arts, mathematics, science and social studies.

Project PLAN was conceived by Dr. John C. Flanagan, and to some extent evolved from the findings of Project TALENT, a large-scale, long-range project involving the collection of comprehensive information about education in the United States. Project TALENT involved the testing of a sample of 440,000 students in 1,353 secondary schools in all parts of the country in March 1960, with subsequent follow-up studies.

PREFACE

Through Dr. Flanagan's efforts, Project PLAN was brought into being in February 1967 as a joint effort of the American Institute for Research, Westinghouse Learning Corporation, and thirteen school districts.[1] Dr. Flanagan has continued to direct the developmental and research work on Project PLAN since that date. Assisting in the developmental work of Project PLAN has been Dr. Robert F. Mager, who is well known for his book *Preparing Instructional Objectives.*[2] Dr. Mager's philosophy was followed in the development of the objectives in these volumes.

The objectives in these volumes, then, have originated from teachers and have been tried out in schools. We wish to acknowledge the efforts of the teachers (their names are listed below) who were assigned by their school districts to work for a year at the American Institute for Research in Palo Alto. Without their contributions these volumes of objectives would not have been possible.

Archdiocese of San Francisco, Department of Education: Sister Maura Cole, Marian Bonnet, Janice Edminster, Sister Charlene Foster, Sister Bernice Heinz, Sister Patricia Hoffman, Sister Mary Vincent Gularte, Sister Anita Kelly, Sister Jeanne Marie Sosic

---

1. Archdiocese of San Francisco, Department of Education, San Francisco, California; Fremont Unified School District, Fremont, California; San Carlos Elementary School District, San Carlos, California; San Jose Unified School District, San Jose, California; Santa Clara Unified School District, Santa Clara, California; Sequoia Union High School District, Redwood City, California; Union Elementary School District, San Jose, California; Bethel Park School District, Bethel Park, Pennsylvania; Hicksville Public School District, Hicksville, New York; Penn Trafford School District, Harrison City, Pennsylvania; Pittsburgh Public Schools, Pittsburgh, Pennsylvania; Quincy Public Schools, Quincy, Massachusetts; Wood County Schools, Parkersburg, West Virginia.
2. R. F. Mager, *Preparing Instructional Objectives* (Palo Alto, Calif.: Fearon Publishers, 1962). The cooperating school districts furnished classroom teachers each year from 1967 through June 1970 to develop the objectives and to prepare the Teaching-Learning Units that enable students to accomplish the objectives. These teachers worked under the supervision of American Institute for Research and Westinghouse Learning Corporation professional personnel. The director of these activities was Dr. William M. Shanner. At the end of each year the teachers returned to their respective school districts to initiate the instructional programs organized from the objectives.

PREFACE

Bethel Park School District: Lora Moroni, Gordon Lepri, James Johnson, Judith Andrews, Flora Belle Faddis, David Loadman, Mary Lou Ertman, Roger Johnson, Robert N. Manson, Anna Marie Kerlin, Frances Chase, Robert M. Caldwell

Fremont Unified School District: Lyndall Sargent, Gail Pagan, Rex W. Estes, Caroline Breedlove, Monique Lowy, Charles Swanson, Eileen Trefz, Robert Fairlee, Beverly Ulbricht, Forrest W. Dobbs, Roy C. Fields, Bertram K. Robarts

Hicksville Public School District: Elayne Kabakoff, Richard C. Leuci, Terrence Boylan, Janet Findlay, Willard Prince, Edward Albert, Phyllis A. Kabakoff, Lawrence Dauch, Gerald Shanley, Marjorie Giannelli, Tom Bannan, Gerard F. Irwin

Hughson Union High School District: Warren Green

Penn-Trafford School District: Gary Fresch, Mary Ann Kovaly, Michael Demko, Jack Reilly, Victor Bohince, David Garvin, La-Velle Hirshberg, R. Bruce Robinson

Pittsburgh Public Schools: Ann Mulroy, Jean Brooke, Kenneth Fraser, Shirley Fullerton, Ruth Aaron, Donald Coudriet, Cecilia Sukits, Carmen Violi, Samuel D. Martin, Paul J. Schafer, Mary South, Patricia Sellars

Quincy Public Schools: Jean Ann MacLean, Priscilla A. Dauphinee, Francis Keegan, Katherine Norris, Dennis Carini, Richard Russell, Stephen Fishman, Jack K. Merrill, Marcia A. Mitchell, Robert J. Mattsson, Margaret E. Flynn

San Carlos Elementary School District: Helen Dodds, Natalie Klock, Edith Bryant, Maxine Ross, Elizabeth Movinski, Martha A. Elmore, Charles B. Whitlock, Betty Lee, Lee G. Jensen

San Jose Unified School District: Allaire Bryant, Rise Berry, Hal Garrett, Kathy Roberts, William Harvel, Judy Opfer, Judi Wells, Don Crowell, Oran T. Adams, Marilyn D. Johnson, Alice S. Anderson, Sylvia Atallah

Santa Clara Unified School District: Nancy Wylde, Ruth Hessenflow, Arthur A. Hiatt, Herman Neufeld

PREFACE

Sequoia Union High School District: Gale Randall, Rex Fortune, Robert W. DuBois

Union School District: Jo Ann Risko, Peggy Schwartz, Rose Yamasaki, Glenn Moseley, Sue Coffin, Tod Hodgdon, Barbara S. Donley, Frank Kelly

Wood County Schools: Roberta Adkins, Mary Rector, Larry Myers, Virginia Haller, John Hoyes, Connie Chapman, Ada Ardelia Price, David V. Westfall, Nancy M. Rice, John W. Apgar

In addition, the contributions of the following persons should be acknowledged. Mary June Erickson, language arts; Josephine J. Matthews, Dr. Marie Goldstein, and Dr. Gordon McLeod, mathematics; Marvin D. Patterson, science; Dr. Vincent N. Campbell, social studies; Sarah M. Russell, primary; Katheryn K. Woodley, Dr. Mary B. Willis, Debbra D. Michaels, performance standards; and Dr. Helen D. Dell, editorial

Final acknowledgment should go to those who use the objectives in these volumes. Objectives alone, an educational program do not make. They provide at best only a framework. The responsibility for the learning must rest on the student, guided by the teacher, and supervised by the school administration.

William M. Shanner

Palo Alto, California
December 15, 1970

INTRODUCTION

Although these volumes are mainly self-explanatory, the reader may find helpful the information that follows. The organization of the objectives is discussed, terms are defined, and the numbering system is clarified.

When a text is made up of many small parts, the constraints of print mean that each item has a fixed position on a page and within a volume, a position that establishes a sequential relationship with all preceding and following items regardless of whether such a relationship is logical or intentional. Since behavioral objectives may potentially be arranged in so many ways, it is important to understand how this collection is arranged and organized to avoid any unwarranted assumption that a prescriptive sequence is being suggested.

The objectives have been organized into four volumes, based on a natural, though often overlapping, grouping of the four major subject areas: language arts, social studies, mathematics, and science. Each volume ranges from Grade 1 through Grade 12. This arrangement is based on the needs of teachers and curriculum designers to perceive the span of a particular subject over the school years. An equally good argument can be made for presenting all the material across subjects for a single age level in one volume to emphasize the interrelatedness of the disciplines. The drawback of this format lies in the wide variations of curricula chosen in different local situations for a given age group. Subject-focused volumes, therefore, seem to be the most useful, with cross-referencing and cross-indexing to relate the subject areas.

Although each volume covers the traditional period from Grade 1 through Grade 12, grouping of objectives into single grade levels is inappropriate, again because of the flexibility of modern curriculum design. Instead, the objectives within each volume have been grouped according to Primary, Intermediate, and Secondary levels. The objectives in these groups overlap to some extent, but use of the three designations divides the objectives into sections of manageable size.

INTRODUCTION

These three groups, or levels, may be roughly defined as follows:

Primary: Primary refers to Grades 1 through 3 and covers the material that, in most cases, is presented in these three years. Some readiness material is included that covers preschool years. The more advanced material may be applicable to the Intermediate level; some objectives from the Intermediate level may be appropriate for late Primary.

Intermediate: Intermediate refers to the years usually included in Grades 4 through 8. Once again, this decision is arbitrary; curricula for Grades 7 and 8 are sometimes closely related to high-school studies. Where a junior high school includes Grades 7, 8, and 9, the Intermediate and the Secondary objectives need to be considered selectively.

Secondary: Secondary designates high school, from freshman through senior years. The material presumes that the student has covered the work included in the earlier grades. There is little or no re-presentation of review topics, nor are there objectives designed for remedial work.

Within subject areas there are many ways to subdivide material. It is important to have enough subdivisions to be meaningful and yet not so many that overlapping and confusion result.

The following lists show the topics selected for each volume.

LANGUAGE ARTS
- Listening Skills
- Speaking Skills
- Reading Skills
- Writing Skills
- Grammar Skills
- Study Skills
- Personal Communication and Development Skills
- History and Dialectology
- Classification, Interpretation, and Analysis of Literary Forms
- Original Writing
- Oral and Dramatic Interpretation
- Critical Analysis of Media

INTRODUCTION

SOCIAL STUDIES
- History
- Sociology and Anthropology
- Political Science
- Geography
- Economics
- Psychology and Philosophy
- Social Studies Inquiry Skills

SCIENCE
- Life Science
  - Biology (at secondary level only)
- Physical Science
  - Chemistry (at secondary level only)
  - Physics (at secondary level only)
- Earth Science
- Science Inquiry Skills

MATHEMATICS
- Analysis of Number and System
- Operations: Numerical and Algebraic
- Operations: Graphics
- Geometry
- Measurement and Probability
- Sets and Logic
- Problem Solving

The topics are useful here, but their sequence has no special significance. A sequence that appears logical to one curriculum designer may seem totally illogical to another. Printed material can never embody the flexibility that is possible in instruction. For example, in *Social Studies* the major topics occur in the same sequence through Primary, Intermediate, and Secondary levels. This sequence by no means implies that history should precede political science or economics in any one of these levels, since much instruction proceeds concurrently in various topics as well as in subject areas.

Another problem in writing objectives lies in breaking the material into appropriate learning "chunks." An objective can be so broad that it is meaningless, or it can represent such a small sample of behavior that the instructional program appears to proceed at a snail's pace.

INTRODUCTION

Behavioral Objectives: A Guide to Individualizing Learning approaches this quandary by selecting major benchmarks in student progress. These have been designated Terminal Objectives; subsumed under these, Transitional Objectives group the Terminal Objectives into smaller units.

A Terminal Objective represents a major growth point in student progress, the culmination of work done over a period of time. It can be tested through a project undertaken by a student as in a social-studies investigation, or it may be measured by a test that presents a variety of problems as defined in the objective.

Transitional Objectives lead the student to mastery of the Terminal Objective. Decisions regarding the amount to be mastered in a Transitional Objective may appear to have been made on an arbitrary basis. Sometimes small categories have been grouped into an objective that represents a fairly large area of behavior. Other objectives may seem overly small. Once again, it must be emphasized that these objectives serve as guidlines, not as prescriptions.

Numbering System: Each Terminal Objective is identified by a subject-area designator—LA for language arts, SS for social studies, MA for mathematics, and SC for science—and a three-digit number. The numbers begin with 005 and continue at intervals of five, with a few exceptions, so that new Terminal Objectives can be inserted without rearrangement of the numbering system. In final editing of these volumes such interpolations were made, and the new numbers were assigned sequentially. In each subject area Primary begins with 005, Intermediate with 200, and Secondary with 500. Since numbers were assigned after the objectives were assembled, they do not represent a prescribed sequence.

For those who are interested in making a more comprehensive numbering system, a two-decimal designator can be added for each of the Transitional Objectives that follows a Terminal Objective. (In the present collection no set of Transitional Objectives exceeds 99.) For computer purposes, each of the lettered subject-area designators may be assigned a number: 1, 2, 3, 4.

In this way a six-digit code can be constructed to identify any objective by subject area or by age group. Addition of a seventh digit would permit identification of the cognitive level as well.

INTRODUCTION

Cross-references: To show the interrelatedness of these objectives, some cross-referencing has been indicated by numbers in parentheses that refer to Terminal Objectives. The letter designator shows whether reference is made to an objective in the same area or to one in another subject area. These cross-references can only suggest the wide possibilities of relating various topics.

Cognitive level: Behavioral objectives are often criticized for their seeming triviality and the fact that many of them call upon memorization and application of learned facts. In an effort to test the objectives in these volumes, a modified approach to Bloom's *Taxonomy of Educational Objectives, Cognitive Domain* was applied, using six cognitive levels. This evaluation proved a revealing indication of how well these objectives are distributed among the cognitive levels. For this reason the cognitive level has been included and is indicated by a roman numeral following each objective.

Each Terminal Objective has been carefully phrased to indicate specifically the cognitive level expected. Transitional Objectives do not follow a rigidly consistent pattern, but wherever possible the verbs were selected from the lists related to the cognitive levels.

The following phrases and verbs have been used:
LEVEL I: KNOWLEDGE. Emphasis is on recall, whether of specifics or universals. Terminal Objective: Show that you know (about) . . .

Transitional Objectives for Level I for the most part use the following verbs: answer questions, choose, define, finish, complete, follow directions, identify, indicate, label, list, locate, match, select.

LEVEL II: COMPREHENSION. Emphasis is on grasp of meaning, intent, or relationship in oral, written, graphic, or nonverbal communication. Terminal Objective: Show your understanding of . . . (by) . . .

In Transitional Objectives the following verbs are used: classify, compare the importance of (not just *compare,* which is Level VI), derive, describe, estimate, expand, explain, express, interpret, measure, put in order, recognize, suggest, summarize, trace, convert, add, balance, calculate, compute, divide, factor, multiply, subtract, write numerals.

INTRODUCTION

LEVEL III: APPLICATION. Emphasis is on applying appropriate principles or generalizations. Terminal Objective: Show that you can use or apply . . .

Transitional Objectives draw mainly on these words: apply, compute, construct, make, draw, demonstrate, differentiate, discuss, express in a discussion, find, use, collect information, keep records, participate, perform, plan, predict, prepare, present, solve (word problems, problem situations), use.

LEVEL IV: ANALYSIS. Emphasis is on breakdown into constituent parts and detection of relationships of the parts and of the way they are organized. This level is often an aid to comprehension or a prelude to evaluation. Terminal Objective: Demonstrate your ability to perceive . . . (the parts of/relationship between) . . . (Words in parentheses can be implied or stated in terms of specifics.)

Transitional Objectives draw from this list: analyze, debate, determine, differentiate, form generalizations, deduce, draw conclusions, make inferences, organize.

LEVEL V: SYNTHESIS. Emphasis is on putting together elements or parts to form a whole not clearly there before the student performance. Terminal Objective: Demonstrate your ability to combine concepts, principles and generalizations.

Transitional objectives usually include one of the following verbs: combine and organize, design, develop, produce, write (an original composition).

LEVEL VI: EVALUATION. Emphasis is on values, making qualitative or quantitative judgments with criteria from internal or external sources and with standards. Terminal Objective: Make a judgment on . . . or involving . . .

Transitional Objectives are built around these verbs: compare (and contrast), make a decision, decide, evaluate.

The reader or user is encouraged to criticize the application of cognitive levels in relation to accuracy of application as well as to appropriateness for the particular topic or age group. Like all other facets of these objectives, the listing of cognitive level is designed to stimulate thought regarding the instructional program.

PRIMARY

LISTENING SKILLS

LA 005 Show that you can follow oral directions. III

Follow directions for drawing pictures. I

Follow directions in dictating a sentence to the teacher describing a picture, an object, or an experience. I

Follow directions in making a copy of your own name from a model. I

Follow directions in arranging pictures and objects in a predetermined order. I

Follow directions for playing games. I

Follow directions in marking worksheets. I

Follow oral directions involving several steps. I

LA 010 Show that you can differentiate between sounds. III

Identify loud and soft sounds. I

Identify human and nonhuman sounds. I

Indicate recognition of a variety of rhythms by clapping your hands, clicking your tongue, skipping, hopping, etc., to the beat of the rhythm. I

After you hear a dictated word, pronounce another word that rhymes with it. I

LA 015 Show that you can remember specific information from an oral presentation. I

After listening to a short story, identify the proper sequence of a series of four or five pictures related to the story. I

After listening to a story, identify the events that happened in the beginning, middle, and end of the story. I

After listening to a story, describe the events that happened first, next, and last in the story. II

After listening to a story, match answers with questions on the details. I

After listening to a passage, answer questions about the passage. I

After hearing a passage, identify the events that occurred in the story from a list of given events. I

After listening to a story or report, answer from one to three questions using facts from the story. I (SS 175)

Recognize the main idea in an oral passage that you have just heard. II

Recognize the mood of an oral passage. II

SPEAKING SKILLS

LA 020 Show that you can present ideas orally. III (SS 175)

Describe in your own words how two objects or pictures differ. II (SS 020)

Describe in your own words the probable reactions of persons in pictures and stories. II (SS 155)

Express basic human needs. II (SS 085)

LA 025 Show that you can present descriptions of personal experiences. III

Tell a story about something you have seen, heard, or read. I

Tell about a personal experience. I (SS 010)

PRIMARY

LA 030 Show that you can present ideas effectively to an audience. III (SS 175)

Retell a story that you have read or heard. I

Present an oral report about a story character, identifying the story and the character. Describe the character briefly. III

Present a true adventure or make-believe story to a class or a small group. III

After reading a story, prepare and present a short oral report based on the main idea, the characterization, and/or events in the story. III

Express your ideas on a given subject, using complete sentences and distinct, coherent, and precise speech. II (SS 175)

Write an outline for an interview including the following: the reason for the interview, the topic to be discussed, and specific questions to be asked. III (SS 170)

Conduct an interview, asking questions relevant to the topic and making notes of the answers. III (SS 170)

Express an idea you have chosen, using descriptive words. II

Given an illustration, tell about any action in the picture. I

LA 035 Show that you can participate in group discussions. III (SS 155)

Plan activities for a group discussion. Planning should include: (1) choosing a group leader and (2) setting up questions for discussion or selecting a topic for discussion. III

Demonstrate the ability to (1) take turns in speaking, (2) listen to others when they speak, and (3) stay on the subject while taking part in a group discussion. III

After participating in a group discussion, evaluate the discussion on the basis of techniques and content. VI

READING SKILLS

LA 040 Show your understanding of relationships by identifying objects and classifying them according to size, shape, and number. II (SC 015)

Given an illustration, name at least five objects in the picture. I (MA 005)

Given sets of objects, classify those objects that belong together. II

Given a set of concrete objects, pictures of objects, or letters, identify the one object or picture that is different (in size, shape, or number) by isolating it or marking it. I (SC 015)

LA 045 Show that you know how to follow a left-to-right sequence. I

Given a continuous dotted line moving from left to right and top to bottom, follow the line with a pencil or finger. I

Given a series of pictures, follow the left-to-right sequence with your eyes and/or finger, telling about each picture. I

Given a series of pictures in two or more lines, follow the progression, transferring from the end of the top line to the left side of the next line. Tell about each picture in sequence. I

LA 050 Show that you know the letters of the alphabet. I

Identify uppercase and lowercase letters by name. I

Given the alphabet, name both uppercase and lowercase forms of any five given letters. I

Identify the correct order of the letters of the alphabet. I

PRIMARY

LA 055 Show your understanding of the similarities and differences among sounds. II (SC 010)

Given a group of four or five pictures, recognize pictures of the objects whose names rhyme. II

Recognize words that rhyme. II (LA 190)

Recognize homonyms. II

LA 060 Show your understanding of similarities and differences among visual symbols. II

Given concrete objects, pictures of objects, or letters, match the like objects or pictures (alike by color, size, shape, position, texture, details) by manipulating or marking them. I (SC 015)

Match like letters or words on the basis of shape. I

Classify pictures, objects, or letters on the basis of size, shape, and position. II

Recognize the colors red, blue, green, brown, yellow, orange, purple, and black and call them by name. II

Use descriptive words to create word pictures. III (LA 180)

LA 065 Show that you can apply a sound to its written symbol to read new words. III

Recognize and use the common sounds of consonants. III

Recognize and use the common short and long vowel sounds. III

Recognize and use consonant digraphs. III

Recognize and use vowel digraphs. III

Recognize that doubling final consonants does not change the consonant sound. II

Recognize and use initial and final consonant blends. III

Recognize silent consonants in words. II

Recognize that the final, silent *e* generally gives the preceding vowel a long sound. II

Recognize and use *r*-controlled vowels. III

Recognize and use vowel diphthongs. III

Recognize when vowel and/or consonant combinations have more than one sound. Use these various sounds. III

Use sound-symbol relationships to spell words correctly. III

LA 070 Show that you can use the analysis of word structure to read new words. III

Recognize and use the plural form of nouns. III

Recognize and use the possessive form of nouns. III

Recognize base words when inflectional endings have been added. II

Recognize and use the contracted form of two words. III

Recognize and use the compounded form of two words. III

LA 075 Show that you can recognize and use given aspects of words. III

Identify the meaning or meanings of a given word. I

Recognize synonyms. II

Recognize antonyms. II

PRIMARY

Recognize the correct homonym from a given pair to complete a sentence. (Homonyms must be within the reading vocabulary of the student.) II

Recognize words that describe action, size, color, shape. II

Recognize given structures of grammatical significance (i.e., endings, prefixes, etc.). II

Recognize descriptive words or phrases in a reading selection. II (LA 180)

LA 080 Show your understanding of word forms and sentence patterns by reading orally. II

Recognize given word forms and sentence structure patterns. II

Read a given passage orally, with correct voice intonation, inflection, and phrasing. II (LA 196)

Recognize and use given printing conventions. III

LA 085 Show that you can follow written directions. III (LA 130)

Follow written directions. I

LA 090 Show that you can apply various techniques for reading new words independently. III

Relate a given sound to its written symbol. II (LA 065)

Read new words by applying spelling patterns. III

Read new words by using knowledge of word structure. III (LA 070)

Apply contextual analysis to read new words. III

WRITING SKILLS

LA 095 Show that you can make visually distinct patterns. III

Given the pattern of your name or a single shape, copy the pattern. I

Given an incomplete outline of a picture or letter, complete the outline, using finger, crayon, or pencil. I

Given a repeating pattern of items, complete the last pattern by supplying the missing item or items. I

LA 100 Show that you know the letters of the alphabet. I

Copy uppercase and lowercase letters from a model. I

Match the uppercase and lowercase forms of the letters of the alphabet. I

Write your own first name without using a model. II

Reproduce from memory all twenty-six letters of the alphabet in order. I

LA 105 Show that you can communicate thoughts in complete sentences. III (LA 150)

Copy a complete sentence. I

Copy words, groups of words, and complete sentences. I

Write given sentences from dictation. II

Write phrases that describe location. II (SS 080)

Transform declarative sentences into interrogative sentences. III

Given simple sentences and phrases, write expanded sentences by adding descriptive words. III (LA 180)

Use descriptive words to express an oral or written idea. III (LA 180)

Write sentences using words you have located in a dictionary. III (LA 140)

Grammar Skills

LA 110 Show your understanding of the elements of sentence structure. II (LA 105)

Recognize the subject of a simple sentence. II

Recognize the predicate of a simple sentence. II

Recognize the determiners in a simple sentence. II

Given a sentence with an adjective and a form of the verb *to be,* recognize the adjective. II

Given a list of the five kinds of subjects, recognize the kind of subject used in a sentence. II

LA 115 Show your understanding of common nouns, proper nouns, and pronouns in sentences. II

Recognize the common nouns in a list of words. II

Recognize the use of a common noun and determiner as the subject in simple sentences. II

Recognize the use of a common noun without a determiner as the subject in simple sentences. II

Recognize the proper nouns in a list of words. II

Recognize a proper noun as the subject in simple sentences. II

Identify the personal pronouns. I

Recognize a personal pronoun as the subject in simple sentences. II

Identify the indefinite pronouns. I

Recognize an indefinite pronoun as the subject in simple sentences. II

LA 120 Show that you can recognize and use correct verb forms in sentences. III (LA 105)

Recognize verbs in sentences. II

Recognize the form of a verb. II

Use subject-verb agreement in writing sentences. III

Recognize the forms of the verb *to be* in sentences. II

Use subject-verb agreement in writing sentences containing the present form of the verb *to be*. III

LA 125 Show that you can correctly apply the following: period, question mark, capital letters, and indentation. III

Recognize needs for capital letters involving names of people, names of animals, and the first word of a sentence. II

Recognize that a period belongs at the end of a statement. II

Recognize that a question mark belongs at the end of a group of words that reads as a question. II

Recognize correct punctuation in writing a date. II (LA 150)

Recognize that a comma separates city and state. II (LA 150)

Use capital letters to begin the names of streets, cities, towns, and states. III (LA 150)

PRIMARY

Apply rules of capitalization in writing titles and headings. III

Identify the correct placement of the title of a story. I (LA 185)

Identify the correct way to indent the first sentence of a story. I (LA 185)

Apply rules of capitalization in writing names of holidays. III

Apply rules of capitalization and punctuation in writing and abbreviating titles of people. III (LA 150)

Recognize given printing conventions. II

STUDY SKILLS

LA 130 Show that you know about instructional materials in the classroom. I

Identify visual symbols in classroom materials. I

Locate specified materials in the classroom. I

Identify the following as found in your room: different kinds of worksheets, papers, games, and equipment. I

LA 135 Show that you can use and care for materials and equipment. III

Use correctly a pencil, crayons, paste, paints, scissors, and puzzles. III

Identify and use any of the following items that are found in your room: record player, cassette tape recorder, film loop projector, filmstrip or slide viewer, and language master. III

Follow directions for returning equipment after it is used. I

LA 140 Show that you can use reference sources to locate and use information. III (SS 180, SS 170)

Given a list of words, put the words in alphabetical order according to the first letter of the word. II

Given a list of words in which the first two letters are the same, put the words in order alphabetically. II

Use alphabetical order to locate telephone numbers in a directory. III (LA 145)

Use a table of contents and indices to locate required information. III

After reading a book, prepare and present a report including the title, the author, and the part or parts that you enjoyed. III (LA 195)

PERSONAL COMMUNICATION AND DEVELOPMENT SKILLS

LA 145 Show that you can use the telephone. III

Demonstrate your ability to dial given telephone numbers. III

Explain what to do if you have to report a fire, call the police, or ask for a doctor. II

Describe the difference between good and bad telephone manners. II

Record a telephone message. III

Locate telephone numbers in a directory. III

LA 150 Show that you can write friendly letters. III (LA 105, LA 125)

Identify the five parts of a friendly letter: heading, greeting, body, closing, and signature. I

Using a model, write an invitation, a friendly note, or a thank-you letter including the greeting, the body, and the closing. III

Apply rules of capitalization in writing the greeting of a letter. III

Apply rules of capitalization in writing the closing of a letter. III

Write a friendly letter, placing the five parts in the correct order. III

Using a model of an addressed envelope, copy the proper form. I

Use correct form to address an envelope. III

HISTORY AND DIALECTOLOGY

LA 155 Show your understanding of language usage by recognizing varieties of expression. II

Identify likeness and difference in pronunciation. I (LA 010)

Recognize differences in pronunciation. II (LA 010)

Identify groups in which you speak differently. I (LA 035)

Recognize more than one word for given meanings. II (LA 075)

CLASSIFICATION, INTERPRETATION, AND ANALYSIS OF LITERARY FORMS

LA 160 Show your understanding of fact and fantasy in literature. II

Recognize an animal who behaves in a way peculiar to animal life. II (SC 005)

Given a story containing real-life and make-believe elements, suggest which elements are real and which elements are make-believe. II

Identify the components of a fairy tale. I

After listening to or reading a story, explain whether the story is true or make-believe. II

LA 165 Show your understanding of a literary selection by reading with 75 percent to 90 percent comprehension. II (LA 090)

After reading a given passage, recognize the main idea. II

After reading a given passage, recognize details. II

Recognize the repetitive portions of a given story. II

Locate a passage that answers a question or contains a specified thought. III (LA 140)

After reading a given passage, describe the sequence of events. II

Recognize the adjective that best describes a given character. II (LA 180)

Present an oral report about a story character, identifying the story and the character and describing him briefly. III (LA 196)

Retell a story that has been seen, heard, or read. I (LA 196)

Recognize descriptive words in phrases and sentences. II (LA 180)

Recognize word pictures in a given poem. II (LA 190)

Recognize facts in an informational reading passage. II (LA 140)

Use contextual analysis to read new words. III (LA 090)

Select the best title for a story from a given list. I

After reading a story, present a short oral report based on the main idea, the characterization, and/or events in the story. III

PRIMARY

LA 170 Show your understanding of contextual clues. II

Read a given passage and make inferences based on details. II

Classify information contained in a reading passage. II (LA 195)

Predict the ending to a reading passage. III

Draw conclusions from information given in a reading passage. II (LA 195)

Recognize cause-effect relationships in a given reading passage. II

Recognize facts in an informational reading passage. II (LA 140)

LA 175 Show that you can apply reading to personal experience. III

After reading a given passage, describe how the passage relates to personal experience. II

After reading a book, prepare and present a report including the title, the author, and the part or parts enjoyed. III (LA 195)

Retell a story you have read or heard and change the ending. II (LA 196)

ORIGINAL WRITING

LA 180 Show that you can use descriptive words or phrases. III

Recognize more than one word to describe something. II

Recognize the adjective which best describes a given character in a story. II

Write descriptive words, phrases, and sentences. III

Apply the use of descriptive words or phrases in creative writing. III

Use a variety of words to express action and sound in speaking and writing. III (LA 030)

Apply the use of alliteration in creative writing. III

Write a real, imaginary, or new name for a given thing. III

LA 185 Demonstrate your ability to combine concepts, principles, and generalizations by writing original stories. V (LA 105)

Write a story you have read or heard and change the ending. III

Given a question asking how or why, write a myth at least one sentence in length. III

Write a make-believe story of at least three sentences with a beginning, middle, and end. V

Write a fictional paragraph about people, animals, places, or things. V

Write a paragraph in which a character is described and developed. V

Write a story that tells who, what, where, when, and why. V

Write a story using story-starter words, phrases, or pictures. V

Given a story starter, write an adventure story using descriptive words. V

Write a true adventure story and tell it to a class or a small group. III (LA 196)

Write a make-believe story. V

PRIMARY

Write a story using a topic you have selected as the main idea. V

Read several stories of fantasy, and then write your own tale of fantasy. V (LA 175)

LA 190 Demonstrate your ability to combine concepts, principles, and generalizations by writing original poems. V

Write a poem of at least one rhyming couplet. V (LA 075)

Write a poem from a given list of topics. V

LA 195 Demonstrate your ability to combine concepts, principles, and generalizations by organizing factual information. V (SS 175)

Write a simple biography, including the person's name and at least two other facts about the person. III

Write a factual paragraph about people, animals, places, or things. V

ORAL AND DRAMATIC INTERPRETATION

LA 196 Show that you can dramatize ideas, emotions, and characters. III

Dramatize the descriptive words and phrases from an oral passage that you have just heard. III

Dramatize the descriptive words and phrases from a passage that you have read. III

Dramatize a given human emotion. III

Dramatize a chosen role in a dramatic play. III

Pretend to be a given animal or story character. III

INTERMEDIATE

LISTENING SKILLS

LA 200 Show your understanding of information presented orally by summarizing and interpreting the content. II

Recognize the main idea and details in an oral presentation. II

Differentiate between fact and opinion in an oral presentation. III

After hearing a one or two paragraph oral selection, answer factual questions about the content of the material. I

Listen to a talk and list the points that should be questioned for supporting evidence. I

After listening to a selection of two or more paragraphs, summarize the material in the correct sequence. II

Given five directions presented orally, follow all directions accurately without asking for repetition. I

Recognize whether the major purpose of an oral presentation is to entertain, inform, or persuade. II

After listening to a political or editorial speech of at least five minutes on television, radio, a record, or tape, describe in two or three sentences (1) the main idea of the speech and (2) two or three subordinate ideas that contribute to the main idea. II (LA 465, SS 425)

Given a written copy of a person-to-person interview you have just heard on tape, recognize comments spoken by the interviewee that are irrelevant to the main topic. II

Recognize controversial topics, opinions, generalizations, and/or arguments presented on a television panel program such as *Meet the Press* or *Face the Nation.* II (SS 315)

Recognize the following signs of bias in a taped radio newscast: loaded words, exaggeration, statements of opinion or statements of prediction presented as fact. II (LA 465)

LA 205 Make a judgment on techniques used by the speaker in an oral presentation. VI (LA 235)

Identify descriptive phrases as describing action, as painting visual pictures, or as denoting sounds. I

Analyze the content of the following parts of an oral presentation: (1) the speaker's purpose, (2) clarity of information, and (3) organization of the material. IV (LA 225)

Evaluate the following parts of a speaker's delivery of an oral presentation: (1) clarity and voice control, (2) posture and action, and (3) eye contact with the audience. VI (LA 225)

SPEAKING SKILLS

LA 210 Show that you can plan and conduct personal interviews. III (SS 430)

Prepare an outline of the questions you would like to ask a person in an interview. III

Conduct an interview with a classmate. Write a report of your interview. III (LA 255)

Conduct an interview with an adult. Present an oral summary of that interview. III (LA 225)

Conduct an interview and write about it for a school newspaper. Include the interviewee's name and at least three facts about his life. III (LA 475)

LA 215 Show that you can make informal oral presentations. III (LA 450)

Review oral presentation skills by explaining how to proceed from your present position or a place that you select, to another place in the school, on the playground, and in the neighborhood. Explain the reverse route. II

Review oral presentation skills by expressing a passage written in formal language in your own words. II

INTERMEDIATE

Review skills for presentation of ideas to an audience by explaining to a group how to perform an activity. II

Demonstrate an accepted procedure for (1) making an introduction and (2) making an announcement. III

Present to the class a selection of prose or poetry that you have written to express a mood. Adjust the tone and rhythm of your voice to the mood of the selection. III

LA 220 Show that you can use techniques for preparing an organized oral report. III (LA 450, SS 430)

Apply the skill of sequencing to organize material for an oral presentation. III (LA 335)

After reading two or more books on a chosen topic, prepare a project that includes a visual model. Present a discussion of the topic. III (LA 235, LA 330)

Prepare an oral report using the following steps. III
1. Choose and limit a subject.
2. Locate information.
3. Take notes.
4. Organize the notes in three sections: one that leads into, one that expands, and one that summarizes the topic.
5. Present the report.

LA 225 Show that you can present an organized oral report. III (LA 345, LA 450)

Present a three- to five-minute talk on a topic you choose. III

After reading a book, present an oral book review. III

After reading an account of a scientific adventure, present an oral report related to the adventure. III

Present orally a project you have prepared. III

Given a controversial topic, make an oral presentation in which you try to persuade others to agree with your point of view. III

Using information you have gathered from readings in a specific category, present your ideas to a small group of friends, neighbors, or family members. III

Prepare and present a three- to five-minute informative talk that will be evaluated on the basis of (1) your posture, (2) your eye contact, (3) the volume of your voice, (4) your speed in speaking (pacing), (5) your pronunciation and enunciation, and (6) your organization of the material. III

LA 230 Show that you can participate in achieving the goals of a discussion group. III

Review the guidelines for a discussion that apply to the participant in a discussion group. I

Review group-discussion techniques expressing your point of view on a topic from your reading in a specific category. II

After reading two selections from a reading list on a specific category, discuss the category, citing examples from your reading. III

Review group discussion techniques by participating in an open-ended group discussion in which no one solution is apparent. Include the following: (1) define the topic, (2) contribute relevant ideas, (3) contribute to the resolution of the problem, and (4) state whether or not you think your contribution was worthwhile. III

LA 235 Show that you can apply techniques for leading a discussion. III (LA 230)

Describe the rules that should be followed by the leader of a discussion group. II

Evaluate the technique used by a discussion leader according to the following criteria. VI
1. Introducing the topic under discussion
2. Refraining from giving personal views
3. Deciding who is to speak
4. Keeping the discussion moving on the topic
5. Giving everyone a chance to speak
6. Summarizing the main points

Demonstrate your ability to lead a discussion group. III

Show that you can use the correct parliamentary procedures in opening and closing a meeting and in introducing and carrying a motion. The following points are suggested rules for conducting a meeting. III

1. The chairman calls the meeting to order.
2. The secretary keeps a record, or minutes, of the business of the meeting.
3. A member secures permission to speak by rising and addressing the chairman.
4. Old business is discussed before new business is introduced.
5. Business is introduced in the form of a motion.
6. Each motion contains only one item of business.
7. A motion must be seconded.
8. The person seconding a motion does not rise or address the chairman.
9. After a motion is seconded, it is discussed and voted upon. It is carried if a majority of members vote in favor of the motion.
10. Members are nominated for office by a nominating committee or by individual members. Officers are elected by vote.
11. A meeting may be adjourned after a motion to adjourn is made and carried; if all business is completed, the chairman may adjourn the meeting.

reading skills

LA 240 Show your understanding of the structure and meaning of words and phrases by relating them to contextual uses. II

Identify homonyms in a given selection. I

Identify antonyms in a given selection. I

Given two words of identical or somewhat similar pronunciation, recognize the word to be used in a given sentence. II

Given two words of identical or somewhat similar pronunciation, recognize the word to be used in a given sentence. II

Given a word or group of words in context, recognize which of the following context clues are given for those words: (1) definition, (2) explanation, (3) opposite idea, or (4) example. II

Demonstrate ability to use words or phrases to convey exact meanings. III

Recognize the technical vocabulary in a given scientific selection. II

LA 245 Show that you can use structural analysis to recognize and use the correct forms of words. III

Review structural analysis by recognizing the following structures of grammatical significance. II
(1) endings: -ed, -ing, -s, -er, -est
(2) plurals: -s, -es, -ies, -ves, variants

Demonstrate ability to use structural analysis to read new words. III

Recognize the written form of a given word. II

Given a group of sentences in which one word in each sentence is incomplete and given a list of suffixes and prefixes, select the appropriate affix to complete the word. II

Given a list of words with affixes, recognize the root of each word. II

Revew structural analysis by finding clues to the meaning of a word by recognizing its parts—root, prefix, or suffix. II

Demonstrate the ability to divide words according to the rules of syllabication. III

LA 250 Show that you can apply skills of phonetic and structural analysis to improve your spelling and reading. III

Using a list of at least thirty words that you have at some time misspelled, design at least three methods or systems for mastering the spelling of these words. V

Apply spelling rules for words that double the final consonant before a suffix. III

INTERMEDIATE

In given situations, apply the rule for the correct spelling of words in the following cases. III

1. Words ending in final *y*
2. Words ending in silent *e*
3. Words containing *ie vs. ei*
4. Prefixes to a root word
5. Suffixes to one-syllable words and to words ending in silent *e*
6. The plural of words

Apply spelling rules for words that adhere to the rules relating to the final *e* before a suffix beginning with a vowel and to the final *e* before a suffix beginning with a consonant. III

Apply rules for spelling the contraction of two or more given words. III

Apply rules for spelling words that adhere to the *ie-ei* rule. III

Read the following sets of homonyms and write sentences spelling and using each member correctly. II

1. aisle
isle
2. already
all ready
3. canvas
canvass
4. capitol
capital
5. coarse
course
6. complement
compliment
7. council
counsel
8. ant
aunt
9. herd
heard
10. its
it's
11. principle
principal
12. stationery
stationary
13. they're
there
their
14. to
too
two
15. waste
waist
16. whose
who's
17. your
you're

Read, use, and spell correctly each of the following words. III

1. accept
except
2. access
excess
3. advice
advise
4. affect
effect
5. ally
alley
6. breath
breathe
7. choose
chose
8. cloths
clothes
9. device
devise
10. later
latter
11. lose
loose
12. moral
morale
13. personal
personnel
14. quiet
quite

Given orally words that end in *-sede, -ceed,* and *-cede,* write sentences using and spelling the words correctly. III

Given a list of some of the most frequently misused and misspelled words and phrases, read, use, and spell them correctly. The following is a suggested list of words. III

1. ache
2. all right
3. answer
4. color
5. cough
6. country
7. don't
8. friend
9. knew
10. know
11. minute
12. tired
13. once
14. since
15. straight
16. tear
17. though
18. through
19. trouble
20. where

WRITING SKILLS

LA 255 Show that you can prepare and present ideas in logical form and sequence. III (LA 345)

Write an outline for a given selection to show main ideas and supporting details. III (LA 340)

Given two or more paragraphs, write a topic outline in the correct form using one level of indentation. III (LA 340)

Summarize a scientific article. II (LA 335)

After reading a selection of prose, write a paper of two or more paragraphs related to the selection. III

After reading a selection of poetry involving an historical event, write a newspaper story from the given facts. III (LA 475)

After reading a given literary selection in a specific category, write a review based on your personal reaction to the selection. III (LA 440)

Given an oral or a written passage, summarize the information. II

INTERMEDIATE

LA 260 Demonstrate your ability to combine concepts, principles, and generalizations by organizing sentences and paragraphs to develop a topic. V (LA 345)

Given groups of words, classify each group as a sentence or as a phrase. Then add words to each phrase to make it a sentence. II

Write a paragraph observing the following guidelines. III
1. Select a topic sentence.
2. Write about one idea.
3. Develop sentences in sequence.

Write an organized explanation of a process. III

Write a short composition supporting your opinion on a given subject, or present a short speech supporting your side in an argument on a given subject. III (SS 430)

Write a critical review analyzing a television program or movie with which you are familiar. IV (LA 455)

After drawing a diagram showing the working parts of an original invention, prepare complete and sequential directions for operation of the invention. III (SC 315)

Conduct an interview with a classmate and write a report of your interview. III (LA 210)

From an outline that you have prepared and with notes you have collected, write a report using the following criteria. III (LA 345)
1. Length: between 300 and 500 words
2. Cover topic adequately
3. Include some facts, if possible
4. Provide examples and/or comparisons to help give clear meanings to your sentences
5. Vocabulary, spelling, and punctuation corrected as far as possible
6. Sentences and paragraphs well formed

Write an article for a school newspaper using criteria of effective journalism. V (LA 475)

Grammar Skills

LA 265 Show that you can apply the transformational rules of grammar. III

Given a list of noun phrases, list the possessive form for each phrase. I

Transform a sentence into a noun phrase by putting the adjective between the determiner and noun of the subject. III

Apply comparison transformation to make a complex sentence out of a pair of simple sentences. III

Recognize the eight reflexive pronouns and use them in sentences. II

Spell the vowel sound ē. I

Spell the vowel sound ā. I

Apply negative transformation to make an affirmative sentence negative. III

Given the modals *have, be,* or *do* with the word *not,* rewrite each pair of words as a contraction. II

Transform a statement into a question. Apply the yes/no question transformation. III

Rewrite a sentence that has an adverbial of place in the predicate as a *where* question. II

Rewrite a sentence that has an adverbial of time in the predicate as a *when* question. II

Rewrite a sentence that has an adverbial of manner in the predicate as a *how* question. II

Rewrite a sentence that has an object of a verb in the predicate as a *whom* or *what* question. II

INTERMEDIATE

Rewrite a sentence as a question by replacing the subject with *who* or *what.* II

Given a basic sentence containing a transitive verb, apply the passive transformation and write the passive sentence in finished form. III

Given a sentence with either a transitive or an intransitive verb, tell whether the structure consists of just a verb or of a verb + particle. I

Given a sentence containing a dangling modifier, rewrite it, making the sentence grammatical by changing the matrix from passive to active or from active to passive. II

Given a certain kind of basic sentence, apply the *there* transformation. III

Rewrite two simple sentences as a third sentence by changing one of the simple sentences into a relative clause. II

Rewrite two simple sentences as a third sentence by compounding, using the conjunction *and.* II

Rewrite two simple sentences as a third sentence by compounding, using the conjunction *or.* II

Rewrite two simple sentences as a third sentence by compounding, using the conjunction *but.* II

Given a sentence, tell whether it is (1) declarative, (2) interrogative, (3) imperative, (4) exclamatory. I

Given a group of sentences containing relative clauses, classify them as restrictive or nonrestrictive clauses. II

Given a sentence with a relative clause containing *be* followed by an adverbial of place, rewrite the clause as an adverbial of place by deleting *relative pronoun + tense + be.* II

Given a sentence with a relative clause containing *be* + *ing,* rewrite the clause as an *ing* phrase by deleting *relative pronoun* + *tense* + *be.* II

Given a sentence with a passive relative clause, rewrite the clause as a participial phrase by deleting *relative pronoun* + *tense* + *be.* II

Given a sentence with a relative clause containing *be* followed by an adjective, reduce the clause to an adjective by deleting *relative pronoun* + *tense* + *be* and then applying the noun modifier transformation. III

Given a sentence with a nonrestrictive relative clause, rewrite the clause by deleting *relative pronoun* + *tense* + *be.* II

Given a sentence with a relative clause, rewrite the clause as an appositive by deleting *relative pronoun* + *tense* + *be.* II

Given a sentence containing the residue of a nonrestrictive relative clause, apply the sentence modifier transformation. III

When *relative pronoun* + *tense* + *be* has been deleted from a relative clause and all that remains is a single-word *ing* verb or a participle, apply the noun modifier transformation. III

Given an insert and a matrix sentence, rewrite the insert as a subordinate clause by introducing the insert sentence with a word called a subordinator. II

Given certain insert sentences, apply the *nominative absolute* transformation. III

LA 270 Show that you can apply the fundamental rules of grammar. III

Given a simple sentence, recognize the subject and the predicate. II

Given a personal pronoun and a form of *be,* identify a contraction formed by combining them. I

Recognize whether the noun phrase that functions as a subject is a determiner + noun, + proper noun, + personal pronoun, or + indefinite pronoun. II

INTERMEDIATE

Given a sentence containing one or more noun phrases, recognize the function of each noun phrase. II

Identify determiners and tell whether their articles are definite or nondefinite. I

Recognize pre-article as an optional feature of the determiner. Use pre-articles in noun phrases. III

Recognize demonstration in noun phrases. III

Recognize number as an optional feature of the determiner. Use numbers in noun phrases. III

Given a common noun, tell whether the noun is count or non-count. I

Tell whether the verb phrase in a given sentence contains a form of *be* or another verb. I

Given a form of *be* in a sentence, recognize the structure that follows as a noun phrase, adjective, or adverbial of place. II

Write sentences from strings of morphemes containing *be* + *ing*. III

Write sentences from strings of morphemes containing *have* + participle. III

Write sentences from strings of morphemes containing tense + modal. III

Given a list of simple sentences containing adverbials, describe each adverbial as an adverbial of place, of manner, or of time. II

Given a group of sentences containing verbals, tell whether the verb in the verbal is transitive or intransitive. If it is transitive, name its object. I

Given a group of sentences containing verbals, recognize whether the verb in the verbal is a verb of the *seem* class, a verb of the *become* class, or a *middle* verb. II

LA 275 Show that you can apply the inflectional morphology rules of grammar. III

Recognize the number of morphemes in a given word. II

Given a list of singular nouns, list the noun in the plural form. I

Given a list of noun phrases, list the possessive form for each phrase. I

List the present- and the past-tense forms of *be.* I

List the present-tense forms of verbs (simple and *s* forms). I

List the past-tense forms of regular verbs. I

List the past-tense forms of irregular verbs. I

List the principal parts of regular and irregular verbs. I

Rewrite given verbs in the *ing* form. II

Write sentences from strings of morphemes containing *be* + *ing.* III

Construct words from base + comparative or base + superlative morphemes. III

LA 280 Show that you can apply the derivational morphology rules of grammar. III

Construct nouns from verbs + *er.* Differentiate an adjective + comparatives from a verb + *er.* III

Make adjectives out of certain nouns by adding *ful* to them. Use the adjectives in sentences. III

Make nouns of measurement out of certain nouns by adding *ful* to them. Use the nouns in sentences. III

INTERMEDIATE

Give the meaning "not" to adjectives and adverbs of manner. Reverse the meaning of verbs by adding the morpheme *un*. II

Make verbs from certain adjectives by adding the morpheme *en*-1. Use the verbs in sentences. III

Make adjectives from certain nouns by adding the morpheme *en*-2. Use the adjectives in sentences. III

Make an adverb of manner from an adjective. Use the adverb in a sentence. III

Make adjectives from certain nouns by adding the *ly*-2 morpheme. Use the adjectives in sentences. III

Construct adjectives from base words by adding either the suffix *able* or *ible*. III

Construct adjectives from base words by adding either the suffix *ent* or *ant*. III

Construct nouns from words by adding either the suffix *ence* or *ance*. III

Identify words that end in the suffix *ate* as either nouns, adjectives, or verbs. I

Construct nouns from given words by adding the suffix *ion*. III

Rewrite certain nouns as adjectives by adding the morpheme *y*. II

Use the morphemes *be, over,* and *under* to construct new words. III

Construct nouns, verbs, adjectives, and adverbs of manner by adding derivational morphemes to base words. III

Use the morphemes *ex* and *re* to construct new words. III

Add the morpheme *in* to adjectives and nouns to give the meaning "not". II

Construct abstract nouns by adding the morpheme *ness* to adjectives. III

Construct adjectives by adding the morpheme *less* to certain nouns. III

LA 285 Show that you can write sentences using the basic parts of speech correctly. III

Recognize nouns, verbs, adjectives, and adverbs by their use in sentences. II

Identify the plural of a given singular noun. I

List the singular possessive and plural possessive forms of nouns. I

Recognize nouns used as direct objects. II

Recognize predicate nouns or linking-verb complements. II

Recognize nouns by suffix endings. II

Demonstrate the use of noun markers in written work. III

Given a list of nouns, classify them as either specific or general nouns. II

Write sentences using personal pronouns as subjects and as linking-verb complements. III

Write the singular, past, and participle forms of regular and irregular verbs. Use each form in a sentence. III

Demonstrate ability to use the correct form of the verbs *draw, fly,* and *blow* in written or oral expression. III

Write sentences using correctly the comparative and superlative forms of adjectives, including the irregular forms of *good, bad, many,* and *little.* III

INTERMEDIATE

In written and oral work, demonstrate ability to use the correct forms of *sit, set, lie, lay, learn,* and *teach.* III

In written and oral work, demonstrate ability to use the correct forms of *tear, wear, fall,* and *swim.* III

Write sentences using personal pronouns as direct objects. III

Write sentences using possessive pronouns correctly. III

Write sentences using indefinite pronouns as substitutes for nouns. III

Recognize verbs and verb phrases in a sentence or group of sentences. II

Differentiate between action verbs and linking verbs. III

Write sentences using single and multiple auxiliaries. III

Write the plain, singular, past, and participle forms of regular and irregular verbs. Use each form in a sentence. III

Review structural analysis by describing the meanings of the verb suffixes *-ize, -fy* (or *-ify*), *-ate,* and *-en.* Use the verb suffixes to form words. III

Review structural analysis by using the verb prefixes *en-, em-, be-,* and *re-* to form new words. III

Recognize suffixes and prefixes that act as adverb signals. II

Write sentences using comparative and superlative forms of adverbs. III

Identify the adverbs in a given sentence. Tell whether the adverbs tell how, when, or where. I

Recognize fixed and movable adverbs. Use each type of adverb correctly in a paragraph. III

Write sentences using adjectives that come before nouns. III

Write sentences using predicate adjectives (complements). III

Identify suffixes that are adjective markers. I

Recognize prepositions and objects of prepositions in sentences. II

Given sentences in which prepositional phrases have been improperly placed, rewrite the sentences correctly. II

Write prepositional phrases using the correct forms of the pronouns. III

Write sentences using connectives other than the connectives used for compounding. III

Write sentences using interjections. III

Demonstrate how to use antonyms and prefixes to give words opposite meanings. III

LA 290 Show that you can write sentences using various types of sentence structure. III

Given a declarative sentence (statement), recognize the complete subject and the complete predicate. II

Given a declarative sentence, recognize the simple subject (headword in the subject) and the simple predicate (headword in the predicate). II

In a question or inverted declarative sentence, recognize the complete subject and complete predicate, and the simple subject and simple predicate. II

In an inverted sentence, apply the rule of subject-verb agreement. III

Write sentences using the N-V (noun-verb) sentence pattern. III

Write sentences using the N-V-N (noun-verb-noun) sentence pattern. III

INTERMEDIATE

Write at least five sentences using the N-LV-N (noun-linking verb-noun) sentence pattern. III

Write sentences using the N-LV-ADJ (noun-linking verb-adjective) sentence pattern. III

Write sentences using compound subjects, or compound predicates, or both. III

Rewrite two simple sentences as one compound sentence. II

Given an affirmative statement, transform it to a negative statement, an affirmative question, or a negative question. III

Classify a given sentence as one of the four types of sentences (declarative, exclamatory, imperative, or interrogative). II

LA 295 Show that you can apply rules of punctuation and capitalization. III

Identify errors in capitalization, punctuation, and spelling in a given business letter. I

Given a sentence containing a connecting word (conjunction, subordinator, or sentence connector), punctuate the sentence, using the generally accepted rules. III

In written conversation, use punctuation and capitalization rules in direct quotations, including broken quotations. III

Given a group of sentences containing quotations that do not have any punctuation or capitalization, use punctuation and capitalization rules in writing the sentences correctly. III

Use capitalization rules in writing correctly a group of given sentences in which capital letters are not used with the first word in each sentence or with words in titles of books, poems, songs, and stories. III

Given a written selection containing errors in composition and mechanics, proofread the material and make the necessary corrections. III

Use commas to set off appositives. III

Write proper adjectives using the correct form. III

Use capitalization in writing proper nouns. III

Given a selection containing regions of countries, trade names, and the names of documents, use rules of capitalization. III

Given a word or words underlined in a sentence, recognize whether the word(s) should be abbreviated, hyphenated, capitalized, or left unchanged. II

Given a written selection, use hyphens between compound words and numbers correctly. III

STUDY SKILLS

LA 300 Show that you can select reading material suitable to your reading level. III

Given a choice of at least five books at different reading levels, apply the rule of thumb in selecting an appropriate book. (Rule of thumb: Open to the middle of the book; if there are five words you don't know on the page, then the book is too difficult.) III

Select and read a short story, poem, and/or articles at an appropriate reading level. Answer questions about details. II (LA 380)

Choose and read at least one book that is appropriate to your reading level. Explain the major ideas and their relationships. II

Determine the suitability of reading material for your purpose, using recognition of sight words and of context clues. IV

INTERMEDIATE

LA 305 Show that you can adjust your reading rate to the purpose and type of material. III

Given a variety of reading materials, such as encyclopedia articles, short stories, poems, and newspaper or magazine articles, demonstrate the ability to adjust your reading rate and technique to the purpose for reading. III

Apply the skills of skimming to locate information about a selected topic. III

Apply reading techniques that help rather than hinder your reading ability and contribute to consistent reading habits. III

Given various selections in history, science, literature, and math, recognize the best approach (rate) and special skills needed in reading the selections. II

LA 310 Show that you can apply reading techniques to take notes. III

Given a reading selection and a specific topic, recognize words, phrases, or sentences that are relevant to the topic. II

Given a paragraph and a topic, recognize the topic sentence of the paragraph. II

Given a topic, a passage and a list of notes, recognize which notes are relevant to the topic. II

LA 315 Show that you can recognize and/or use all parts of a book. III

Given a book containing the following parts, locate each part and identify the page number where each part appears: (1) index, (2) table of contents, (3) list of illustrations, (4) bibliography, and (5) title page. I

Identify the following book parts. I

1. Frontispiece
2. Title page
3. Copyright
4. Dedication
5. Preface, foreword, introduction
6. Acknowledgments
7. Table of contents
8. List of illustrations
9. Text, or body
10. Bibliography
11. Index
12. Appendix

Use an index to identify page numbers of pictures, graphs, or illustrations. III

Use an index to locate subjects. III

Use an index to find topics and subtopics. III

Locate the page number in the table of contents that tells where to find information on a subject or where a story begins. I

LA 320 Show that you can use a dictionary to locate words and to identify the structure and meaning of words. III

Given a list of words whose first three letters are exactly the same, arrange the words alphabetically. II

Given a list of entry words, use guide words to locate each entry word in a dictionary. III

Given a list of derived words that are not entry words, use the dictionary to locate the base (root) word. Use the meaning of the base (root) word and the affixes to suggest the meaning of the derived word. III

Use a dictionary to find the correct meanings of words given in context. III

Use a sample dictionary page to find an example of the following: (1) guide word, (2) entry word, (3) pronunciation key, and (4) definitions. III

Use a dictionary or a glossary to divide given words into syllables. III

Given a group of sentences, each of which contains a word that has the same spelling but a different meaning in each sentence, locate in a dictionary the definition of the word as it is used in each sentence. I

Use a dictionary to find the syllables, pronunciation, parts of speech, meaning, and synonyms for a given word. III

INTERMEDIATE

Use guide words for finding dictionary entries quickly and efficiently. III

Find prefix and suffix entries in the dictionary. Use the entries to form new words. III

Use a dictionary to find the meanings of common idioms. III

LA 325 Show that you can find information in the library. III

After choosing a topic and writing at least five questions about the topic, find appropriate materials to answer the questions. III

Given a list of six or more titles of books, locate the titles in the library and recognize them as being fiction or nonfiction. II

Given any subject matter topic, use the card catalogue to locate the topic's call number. III

Given a list of authors' names, demonstrate the ability to locate the names in the card catalogue. III

Given a list of book titles, demonstrate the ability to find the titles in the card catalogue and record their call numbers. III

Given an author's name, find books written by the author and record their call numbers. II

Given a list of titles of books, names of authors of books, and subjects of books, (1) find each title, name of an author, and subject in the card catalogue, (2) record a call number for each book, and (3) find each book in the library. III

After reading a story about a hero in Greek literature, find information about his life. Present another one of the hero's adventures to the class. III

LA 330 Show that you can use reference material to find information. III

Given a list of topics to be found in an encyclopedia, demonstrate the ability to use guide words to locate the topics. III

Given a topic, find it in the index of an encyclopedia. III

Find information about a given subject in an encyclopedia. III

Given a list of guide letters from encyclopedia volumes and a list of topics, identify the volume in which each topic could be found. I

Given a list of topics and an encyclopedia, an almanac, and an atlas, (1) locate each topic, and (2) identify the reference book and the page number where each topic appears. I

Use subheadings in an encyclopedia to locate specific information. III

Find specific information in an encyclopedia, using cross-references. III

Using the reference section of a library, find information in *Readers' Guide to Periodical Literature* and other special references for a report on a given topic. III

From references containing information about a given topic, take notes that tell who, why, what, where, when, and how. III

Use a thesaurus to expand your understanding of words and your vocabulary. III

LA 335 Show that you can find information for summarizing, making generalizations, and identifying conclusions. III

Given a paragraph and a list of generalizations about the paragraph, recognize those generalizations that are true. II

Given a magazine article or other similar source, summarize it briefly. II

Apply the skill of sequencing to organize material for an oral presentation. III

Form several generalizations about a book of your choice. IV

INTERMEDIATE

LA 340 Show that you can prepare various types of outlines. III

Given a topic and supporting details, prepare a word or phrase outline in proper form using one level of indentation. III

Given a short selection, prepare a proper word or phrase outline of the topic and the supporting details, using one level of indentation. III

Write an outline for a given selection to show main ideas and supporting details. III

Given two or more paragraphs, write a topic outline in the correct form using one level of indentation. III

Produce an outline for a report using notes you have collected from various references. V

LA 345 Demonstrate your ability to combine concepts, principles, and generalizations by producing a factual report from notes and an outline. V

Take notes from an oral or written source. III

Given a list of references to books, magazines, personal interviews, and encyclopedias, put the references in correct bibliographic order and form. II

Suggest a topic for a report that informs, entertains, or presents an argument. II

Personal Communication and Development Skills

LA 350 Show your understanding of appropriate and inappropriate forms of conversation. II

Identify the basic elements of courtesy that are desirable in person-to-person conversations, group conversations, and telephone conversations. I

Differentiate between acceptable and unacceptable conversations and develop guidelines for improving your own conversation. V

LA 355 Show that you can write friendly and business letters using the correct format. III (LA 295)

Identify the formats used for a friendly letter, business letter, and for envelopes that go with the letters. I

Demonstrate your skill in writing various kinds of friendly and business letters. III (SS 410)

Review writing friendly letters by writing one to express your ideas, interests, and ideals to a student in another part of the country. III

Write a business letter to request information, to recommend action, or to order something by mail. III

Write a friendly letter that includes the following parts in the correct form: (1) heading, (2) greeting, (3) body, (4) closing, and (5) signature. III

Write a main address and a return address on an envelope using the correct form. III

Write a business letter that includes the following parts in the correct form: (1) heading, (2) inside address, (3) formal greeting, (4) body, and (5) closing signature. III

Identify errors in capitalization, punctuation, and spelling in a given business letter. I

Using the correct capitalization and punctuation, write a business letter of order, placing the (1) heading, (2) inside address, (3) greeting, (4) body, (5) closing, and (6) signature in correct position. III (LA 295)

Using correct format, capitalization, and punctuation, write a business letter of adjustment and address the envelope for the letter. III (LA 295)

INTERMEDIATE

LA 360 Show that you can use skills of nonverbal communication. III

Given three means of nonverbal communication (pictures, objects, and gestures) and an idea to communicate, predict the ease or difficulty of each and the effectiveness of each. III

Using symbols that you have found or developed, visually communicate an idea or feeling to another person so that he can state the idea or feeling verbally. III

Develop visual signs that communicate information to large groups of people. V

Find an art print, picture, or photograph on a topic of your choice. Explain how your example illustrates that topic. II

Produce one of the following forms of nonverbal communication—painting, piece of sculpture, drawing, collage, photograph, movie—to express a feeling, an attitude, or an idea on a specific category. V

Develop an original project that expresses your feeling about a specific category in literature. V (LA 380)

HISTORY AND DIALECTOLOGY

LA 365 Show your understanding of Latin and Greek prefixes by deriving the meaning of words. II (LA 280)

For each of the following prefixes of opposition, write three sentences using three words that derive a part of their meaning from the prefix. III

1. anti-
2. contra-
3. counter-
4. non-
5. un-
6. in-
7. mis-

For each of the following prefixes of separation, write three sentences using three words that derive a part of their meaning from the prefix. III

1. ab-
2. de-
3. dis-
4. ex- or ec-
5. se-

For each of the following Latin prefixes, write three sentences using three words that derive a part of their meaning from the prefix. III

1. ad-
2. inter-
3. post-
4. pre-
5. ante-
6. pro-
7. re-
8. sub-
9. trans-
10. tele-
11. intro-
12. ob-
13. per-

For each of the following Latin and Greek prefixes, write two sentences using two words that derive a part of their meaning from the prefix. III

1. circum-
2. peri-
3. con-
4. com-
5. co-
6. sym-
7. syn-
8. lux-
9. luc-
10. photo-
11. magni-
12. mega-
13. multi-
14. poly-
15. omni-
16. pan(to)-
17. prim-
18. proto-
19. super-
20. ultra-
21. hyper-

Define each of the following Latin and Greek numerical prefixes. I

1. uni-
2. mono-
3. semi-
4. hemi-
5. demi-
6. sept-
7. hept(a)-
8. cent(i)-
9. quin-
10. pent(a)-
11. du(o)-
12. bi-
13. tri-
14. quad-
15. tetra-
16. octo-
17. octa-
18. sex-
19. hex(a)-
20. dec(a)-
21. mill(i, e)-

LA 370 Show that you can trace the history of a linguistic form (word). III

Given a list of English words of foreign origin, find their meaning and the meaning of related words from the root of the original word. (For example, *aud* means "hear" in Latin; in English we have the words *audience, auditorium,* and *audible.*) II

INTERMEDIATE

Given a list of words, identify words we use that are borrowed from a language other than English. I

Given two columns of words, match words from one column with the appropriate words from the other column to form compound words. I

Give an example of each of the following sources of words: (1) slang, (2) blended words, (3) words formed by combining the first letter of each word of a phrase, and (4) words derived from names of famous people. II

Explain the increased use of slang and its influence on language. II

Recognize new words that are formed from existing elements to meet new needs. II

Explain the effect of technology on the English language. II

Recognize the ways in which dialects differ. II

Explain how vocabulary choices are influenced by age, sex, education, occupation, and origins. II

Identify six types of "Americanisms" that have entered the English language and give examples of each type. Identify the ways in which each of these types entered the language. II

List five methods by which new "Americanisms" are being coined. Give three examples of relatively new words for each method you name. II

LA 375 Show your understanding of regional differences in vocabulary, grammar, and punctuation. II

Discuss how United States regional dialects change in relation to population movement, geographical isolation, and economic development. III (SS 245, SS 250)

Given a list of words, recognize words that have the same meaning but are formed from different dialects. II

List four publications by Noah Webster that helped to standardize the American language. Tell three reasons for the wide circulation accorded his books. I

Explain the relationship between the English colonies and the Mother Country (later the United States and Great Britain) as reflected in their attitudes toward each other's use of the English language during the 17th, 18th, 19th, and 20th centuries. II (SS 210)

CLASSIFICATION, INTERPRETATION, AND ANALYSIS OF LITERARY FORMS

LA 380 Show your understanding of genre by classifying literary selections. II

Given a list of statements describing different kinds of stories, identify statements that describe most myths. I

Given a list of statements describing different kinds of stories, identify statements that describe most folktales. I

Given a list of statements describing different kinds of stories, identify statements that describe most tall tales. I

Given a limerick and several other poems, recognize the limerick. II

Given a list of statements describing different kinds of stories, identify statements that describe most fables. I

Given a list of statements describing different kinds of stories, identify statements that describe biography and statements that describe historical fiction. I

INTERMEDIATE

Given a portion of a literary selection, classify the portion under one of the following: fable, folktale, myth, biography, tall tale, or historical fiction. II

Given descriptions of different kinds of literature, recognize descriptions of the short story. II

Explain the differences between a play and a skit. II

Classify a given selection of nonfiction as belonging to one of the following categories: newspaper or periodical article, essay, biography, autobiography, or scientific writing. II

Recognize ballad stanzas by the following characteristics. II
1. Lines 2 and 4 rhyme.
2. Odd-numbered lines have four accented syllables.
3. Even-numbered lines have three accented syllables.

Recognize free verse by its irregular rhythm. II

LA 385 Show your understanding of the main and supporting ideas in literary selections. II (LA 335)

Given a short selection with the topic stated, recognize supporting details from a list. II

Summarize the main ideas in each of three selections (one oral, one visual, and one written) that you have chosen. II

Describe the main ideas and supporting details of a book you have read. II

Given a short reading selection, the main idea of the selection, and a list of details, recognize the details that most directly support the main idea. II

Describe the main idea of a fiction book of your choice. Explain the details that most directly support the main idea. II

Given a list of details about a reading selection that has an obvious conclusion, recognize the details that support the conclusion. II

Recognize several details that support the conclusions you have made from reading a book of your choice. II

Given a paragraph and list of topics, recognize the topic of the paragraph. II

Recognize which sentences in a paragraph are related to the topic of the paragraph. II

From a reading list on a given category, read a short story, an essay, a book, a play, or a poem; suggest examples of a specific topic developed in that selection. II

Find in a library one or two selections related to a specific category. Read the selections, and as you read, recognize passages that illustrate the theme. Include the passages in a journal. II (LA 325)

Given a selection of literature related to a specific category, explain how the selection illustrates that category. II

After reading a poem, answer specific questions about its content. I

Locate articles in the various sections of a newspaper. Answer questions about each of these articles. I

LA 390 Show your understanding of the personality traits of literary characters. II (SS 395)

Given a short selection, recognize the words and/or phrases in the selection that describe traits (such as honesty, kindness, impatience) of the main character in the selection. II

Recognize words that describe the traits of one of the characters in a book of your choice. Describe a situation in which the character displays the traits you have listed. II

Describe orally or in writing the feelings of one or more of the major characters in a fictional selection. Explain why you think they behaved and felt the way they did. II

INTERMEDIATE

LA 395 Show your understanding of literary selections by making inferences based on details. II

After reading a fictional selection at the appropriate reading level, predict future consequences. III

Given a selection of two or more paragraphs and a list of implied statements, recognize statements about the selection that are valid. II

Recognize several facts that are implied but not stated in a book of your choice. II

Given an unfinished selection, predict a future event on the basis of previous events in the selection. III

After reading up to the last chapter in a book of your choice, predict what you believe will be the outcome. III

Analyze a given selection by inferring the author's intent and by drawing conclusions from the evidence presented. IV

Analyze a selection to find the author's hidden meaning by identifying what is implied. IV

LA 400 Show your understanding of cause and effect relationships in literary selections. II

Recognize in a given reading selection, words and/or phrases that demonstrate cause and those that demonstrate effect. II

Given a short reading selection, write a brief paragraph explaining cause-effect relationship from that selection. III

Explain a cause-effect relationship in a book of your choice. II

LA 405 Show your understanding of the setting in literary selections. II

Given a short reading selection and list of statements, recognize the statement that best describes the setting. II

Describe orally or in a paragraph the setting of a book of your choice. II

Explain the effect of the setting (time in history, place, and particular circumstances of the environment) on the principal characters in a given novel or short story from a specific category. II (SS 215, 245)

LA 410 Show your understanding of plot development in literary selections. II

Describe the time, place, characters, and sequence of action in a short story. II

Describe the rising action, climax, and falling action in a given short story. II

In a three-page paper, summarize the main conflict in a novel or a short story of your choice in a given category. In your paper include the underlying causes of the conflict, and the events that contributed to the conflict. Explain the effect of the final resolution of the conflict on each of the principal characters. III (LA 260)

LA 415 Demonstrate your ability to perceive the author's intent and/or point of view in literary selections. IV

Given a short story, an essay, a poem, a book, or a play from a specific category, recognize the author's point of view on a topic. II

Given a short story, an essay, a poem, a book, or a play on a specific topic, describe the way in which the author's point of view is developed. II

Given an editorial, recognize the purpose or purposes (explanation, persuasion, criticism, praise, or entertainment) that the editorial serves. II (LA 455)

LA 420 Demonstrate your ability to perceive mood and tone in literary selections. IV

Given a paragraph and a list of phrases describing mood, recognize the phrase that best describes the mood of the paragraph. II

INTERMEDIATE

Describe in one or more paragraphs the mood of a fiction book of your choice. II

Recognize the particular emotion expressed in a passage. II

Write a short analysis of the technique used by the author to express an emotion in a selection of prose or poetry. IV (LA 260)

Given two passages with the same topic, recognize the words or phrases that are used to change the tone. II

LA 425 Make judgments involving the comparison of reading selections to personal experiences. VI

Explain how a book you have read relates to other selections you have read on the same subject. II

After reading a book at an appropriate reading level, evaluate the validity of the message in terms of personal experience. VI

LA 430 Show your understanding of literary devices in given selections. II (LA 435)

Given a descriptive passage of prose or poetry, recognize the similes. II

Given a reading selection, either poetry or prose, recognize the metaphors. II

Given a variety of poems, recognize those words that demonstrate alliteration. II

Given descriptive words or phrases, pictures, or music, list images brought to mind by each example. I

Recognize examples of metaphor. II

Recognize examples of similes. II

Recognize examples of personification. II

Given a descriptive paragraph, describe the type of space order used (large to small, near to far, top to bottom, etc.) and recognize the words that show the space order. II

Given a narrative paragraph, explain the time order of the actions. II

ORIGINAL WRITING

LA 435 Show that you can use techniques of creative writing. III

Tell whether phrases describe action, paint pictures, or name sounds. I

For each verb in a given list, suggest other verbs that are more descriptive. II

Rewrite sentences by adding adjectives and adverbs. II

After reading a selection that presents suggestions for improving creative writing, apply some of these suggestions to a selection of your own. III

Demonstrate the ability to improve sentences by adding modifiers. III

Summarize the information that should be included when writing the script for a skit. II

Given a noun, suggest modifiers that indicate (1) "which" and then (2) "what kind of." (Include at least one word that tells "which" and at least one word and one phrase that tell "what kind of.") II

Given a verb, suggest a one-word modifier that tells "how" and a phrase modifier that tells "where" to use with the verb. II

Write simple comparisons using metaphors. III

Recognize general and specific statements. II

INTERMEDIATE

Write examples of general and specific statements. III

Given specific statements, rewrite the statements to make them general statements. II

Given general statements, rewrite the statements to make them specific statements. II

In a given passage, recognize the words or phrases that appeal to the five senses (sight, smell, taste, touch, and hearing). II

Write sentences using words that appeal to the five senses (sight, smell, taste, touch, and hearing). III

Write a brief paragraph including words that appeal to as many of the five senses as possible. III

Write a short paper (two pages) about an action or a person, place, or thing of your choosing in which you include impressions, descriptions, and comments based on each of the five senses (sight, smell, taste, touch, and hearing). III

From a reading list on a specific category, choose two selections and recognize impressions, descriptions, and/or comments in each selection that appeal to one of the five senses—sight, smell, taste, touch, hearing. II

Write a comparison of two literary characters from the same selection or from different selections, considering their physical appearance, personality, and personal qualities. III

Using general statements only, write a short paragraph on a subject of your choice. Then rewrite the paragraph, changing all the general statements to specific statements. III

Using specific statements only, write a short paragraph on a subject of your choice. Then rewrite the paragraph, changing all the specific statements to general statements. III

Given introductory sentences from narrative selections, classify the function of each sentence as (1) summarizing some past events as background for the coming story; (2) giving details to create an unusual situation or setting; (3) making a dramatic statement or creating an atmosphere of suspense. II

Write examples of introductory narrative sentences of the following types. III
1. A sentence summarizing some past event as background for a new story
2. A sentence giving details which create an unusual situation or setting
3. A sentence that makes a dramatic statement or creates an atmosphere of suspense

Demonstrate the ability to apply the skills and techniques that are basic to the four forms of written composition: description, narration, exposition, and opinion or argumentation. III

Given examples of closing sentences in narrative passages that serve one of the following functions, recognize the function served. II
1. Expresses a definite emotional response
2. Leads smoothly into the next paragraph, thus serving as a transitional sentence
3. Hints at a subsequent solution to the problem

Write a narrative episode to be evaluated according to the following criteria. III
1. A strong opening sentence
2. Order and relationship of the sentences
3. A closing or summary sentence that completes the action
4. Mechanics of language

Write a descriptive passage for each of the following. III
1. A character's physical appearance
2. A character's attitudes in a particular situation
3. A person's good or bad qualities

Write a paragraph of description placing emphasis on the following. III
1. An introductory sentence giving the point of view
2. A definite space order in the relationship of sentences in the body of the paragraph
3. A summary sentence giving a total impression
4. Mechanics of language

Write a paragraph describing a process or explaining a new term. Criteria for evaluation will include the following. III
1. A clear statement of your purpose in the topic sentence
2. Logical sequence and relationship of explanatory sentences
3. A summary sentence bringing your exposition to completion
4. Mechanics of language

INTERMEDIATE

Using information reading material as your source, suggest an example of each of the following types of expository writing. II
1. An explanation, with a main statement supported by details
2. A definition of a new term
3. Clarification of a process
4. An essay; a person's viewpoint on a topic

Write one paragraph involving argument, such as one concerning a choice between two things you want very much. Criteria will include the following. III
1. A precise statement of your problem in the topic sentence
2. Reasoning logically outlined in the body of the paragraph
3. A concluding sentence giving a final decision
4. Mechanics of language

LA 440 Demonstrate your ability to combine concepts, principles and generalizations by writing original compositions. V

Write a short story that has a beginning, a middle, and an ending. V

Write a short story that has at least one well-developed character. V

Write a short story that has a plot. V

Write a story using word pictures to describe characters, events, and setting. V

Write a story involving a situation portraying emotion, such as anger, joy, or frustration. V

Write a story that includes a dialogue (direct quotations) between at least two people. V

Given the characteristics of a fantasy, write an original fantasy. V

After reviewing selections of poetry on a particular subject, write an original poem. V

Write a script for a play that includes (1) a list of characters, (2) the setting of each scene, (3) dialogue with speakers' actions. V (LA 445)

INTERMEDIATE

Write an original limerick using the following guidelines. V
1. Lines 1, 2, and 5 should rhyme.
2. Lines 3 and 4 should rhyme.
3. Lines 1, 2, and 5 should be longer than lines 3 and 4.

Write an original poem in free verse. V

Using vivid word pictures, write a description of a person, a place, an object, or an event. III

Using fact and fantasy, write a narrative. III

Write your own selection of prose or poetry that expresses how something looks, sounds, acts, and feels. Use specific nouns and descriptive verbs. Modify nouns and verbs with words and phrases. V

Write one to three paragraphs including original examples of metaphor, simile, and personification. III

Given a painting or a picture of a painting, write an original description of the painting using prose or poetry. Include a metaphor, a simile, or personification. V

Given a passage that describes a particular mood, write your own selection of prose or poetry that creates the same mood. Set the tone of your words to fit the mood. V

Given a picture that shows at least one person expressing an emotion, write your own selection of prose or poetry to express the emotions of the person or people in the picture. V

Write an adventure story that includes descriptive and narrative paragraphs. V

Write a character sketch that includes (1) a description of the character and his surroundings and (2) a conversation between the character and another person. III

Write an original plot for the development of a short story. Include at least three related events. V

INTERMEDIATE

Compare and contrast the treatment of a topic in a movie, a television program, or a play with the treatment of the same topic in a written selection. VI (LA 455)

Write a poem, song, story, or essay. V

Write at least two passages vividly describing smells and sounds. III

After reading a selection of literature, write an original composition about the period of time covered in the selection. V

Write an imaginative composition using words that might develop from our language in the future. V

Write a tall tale about a character who works at an occupation that interests you. V

Given a specific situation, write a descriptive paragraph about that situation. III

Pretending to be a well-known person from history or literature, review friendly letter skills by writing a letter in which you tell about some phase of your life. III

Given the characteristics of a myth, write an original myth. V

Given a number of specific items, write an imaginary experience involving those items. V

Write an original couplet. V

Write an original quatrain. V

Write an original haiku verse using the 5-7-5 syllable pattern. V

Write an original tanka verse. V

Write an original verse in one of the simple cinquain patterns. V

Oral and Dramatic Interpretation

LA 445 Demonstrate your ability to combine concepts, principles, and generalizations by developing dramatic techniques. V

Identify important guidelines for participating in a play. I

Given a skit that has been prepared, present the skit to the class. III

Summarize information that should be included when writing a script for a skit. II

Write a script for a play that includes (1) list of characters, (2) setting of each scene, and (3) dialogue with speakers' actions. V

Participate in a play that you or a classmate has written. III

LA 450 Show that you can make a variety of oral presentations. III

Using a selection of literature, prepare and present a choral reading. III

Demonstrate ability to introduce a speaker, giving an introductory remark, some background information about him, and the topic of his speech. III

Present an oral interpretation of a memorized poem of your choice. III

Critical Analysis of Media

LA 455 Show your understanding of the importance of mass media to individuals and to large populations. II

Describe forms of mass media that could be used to inform, persuade, or entertain a large group of people (such as the population of a country) about a given topic. Explain why each medium is more or less useful for this purpose than the other forms. II

INTERMEDIATE

Describe aspects of mass media that some people find useful. Explain how mass media are useful to these people. II

Given an example of a particular person's role in society, explain how mass media could help, as well as harm, this person. II

LA 460 Demonstrate your ability to perceive effects of television. IV

Suggest ways that television could affect a person's family life and his education. II

Explain the difference between a television viewer who controls his television viewing and one who is controlled by his viewing. II

Analyze ten television programs using the following criteria. IV
1. Is there violence in the program?
2. Is there a social message in the program? What is it?
3. Is there a message of personal value in the program?
4. Is there evidence of prejudicial attitudes in the program?
5. Does the program contribute to your intellectual growth?
6. Is the program beneficial mainly as a means of relaxation?

Explain why the following types of television programs often include violence: (1) news, and (2) movies and series, including detective, spy, western, war, horror, and science-fiction formats. II

Write a critical review analyzing a television program or movie with which you are familiar. IV

LA 465 Show that you can differentiate among statements of fact, fiction, and opinion. III

Given a reading selection and a list of statements about the selection, differentiate between statements of fact and statements of opinion. III

Differentiate between fact and opinion in an oral presentation. III

Determine whether the content of a paragraph reinforces the assertion of the paragraph. IV

Analyze a selection for the obvious (and sometimes not-so-obvious) contradictions, errors, exaggerations, and different points of view. IV

Given a news article, an editorial, or some other written work, analyze its viewpoint, bias, and/or objectivity. IV

LA 470 Demonstrate your ability to perceive the techniques and effects of advertising. IV

Given a list of guidelines for producing advertisements, recognize which guidelines apply to the following: (1) television commercials, (2) magazine ads, (3) billboards, and (4) radio commercials. II

From a television radio, billboard, or magazine advertisement, differentiate between information that is implied and information that is stated. III

From a television, radio, billboard, or magazine advertisement, recognize information that is misleading and explain why it is misleading. II

LA 475 Demonstrate your ability to combine concepts, principles, and generalizations by producing a simple newspaper (no less than one page) that includes one article of class (local) interest, one article of school (national) interest, one article of community (world) interest, and one article from each of the following sections: classified, sports, theater-entertainment, editorial, and comics. V

Find information and employment opportunities in newspapers. III (SS 410)

Locate articles in various sections of a newspaper, and answer questions about each of these articles. I

Given a local newspaper, recognize at least one article of local interest, one article of national interest, and one article of world interest. II

INTERMEDIATE

Recognize the following parts of a local newspaper: (1) headline page, (2) sports page, (3) classified section, (4) editorials, and (5) index. II

Write an article for a school newspaper, using the criteria for effective journalism. V

Write and conduct an interview for a school newspaper, including the interviewed person's name and at least three facts about his life. III

Given the lead paragraph from a news story, identify the parts that tell who, what, when, where, and how. I

After reading a selection of poetry involving an historical event, write a newspaper story from the given facts. III

Given a news story and three headlines, recognize the headline that uses the least space in presenting the main fact of the news story. II

Given an editorial, recognize the purpose(s) (explanation, persuasion, criticism, praise, or entertainment) that the editorial serves. II

Given a newspaper review of a book, recording, movie, or television show, determine whether or not the review (1) states an opinion, (2) makes a recommendation, (3) includes basic information, or (4) summarizes briefly. IV

Given examples of classified ads from a newspaper, recognize ads that present all the necessary information. II (SS 410)

LISTENING SKILLS

LA 505 Demonstrate your ability to perceive content and speech techniques by listening to oral presentations. IV

Evaluate the performance of a moderator in a discussion with respect to the following: (1) giving evidence of being well prepared on the discussion topic, (2) asking questions that start a discussion and keep it moving, (3) holding back his own opinion, (4) keeping the discussion to the point and pacing the discussion, (5) bringing the discussion to a conclusion within the allotted time, and (6) summarizing what was discovered or learned during the discussion. VI

In writing and/or discussion, analyze both written and oral presentations for faulty generalizations. IV (SS 425)

SPEAKING SKILLS

LA 510 Show that you can prepare a speech using techniques appropriate to your purpose as a speaker. III (LA 585)

Plan a speech to entertain, inform, or persuade. III

Use appropriate resources to obtain statistics, anecdotes, witticisms, quips, humorous verse, and quotations for use in a speech. III

Write an outline for the body of your speech in one of the following ways: topical order, sequential order, or logical order. III

LA 515 Show that you can use the speech forms and techniques appropriate to your purpose as a speaker. III (LA 585)

Demonstrate four ways to begin a speech. III

Demonstrate four ways to conclude a speech. III

Present orally or in writing a clear, accurate explanation of a given term or process for an audience that is unfamiliar with it. III

SECONDARY

LA 520 Show that you can present a speech or another form of oral presentation using the appropriate techniques. III (LA 585)

Demonstrate voicing techniques in a speech by varying the pitch, volume, and forcefulness of your voice and the rate at which you speak. You should also exercise proper articulation and pronunciation. III (LA 685)

Demonstrate body action and gesture as a means of communication in a speech. III (LA 360)

Demonstrate in a speech at least two methods of eliciting a response from your audience. III

Given a choice of topic, related materials, and a list of procedures, select and present a five-minute speech demonstrating voicing techniques. III (LA 685)

Present an oral explanation in which you include some form of visual aid. The explanation should be understandable to an audience that is unfamiliar with the topic. III

Given a situation in which you are asked to explain how to get from one place to another, present clear directions. They must contain adequate information and be arranged in the proper sequence. III

Prepare a three-minute oral presentation about a personal experience. III

Prepare and present a three- to five-minute speech in which you introduce a speaker to an audience. Your speech must include the following. III

1. The speaker's name and the title of his speech
2. The speaker's background, including place of birth, education, previous jobs held, present status or position, committees served on, articles or books written, and personal facts of possible interest to the audience

LA 525 Show that you can participate in group situations in which personal opinions and values are being expressed. III

Participate in a discussion by showing that you can do the following. III

1. Prepare yourself on the subject so your contributions are worthwhile.
2. Participate in discussion without monopolizing or interrupting.
3. Be tactful in comments.
4. Avoid making comments of little consequence or dwelling on irrelevant ideas.

Demonstrate debating procedures by participating in a debate on a personal or social issue. III

Participate in a debate on any subject of current interest as debater, moderator, or evaluator. An acceptable debate will contain the following. III

1. Evidence that is definite, extensive, pertinent, and convincing
2. Organization that is clear, logical, and strong
3. Analysis that shows a thorough study of the question
4. Refutation that shows the speaker is able to adapt as well as answer and think clearly
5. Delivery that is enhanced by one's personal appearance, voice, articulation, and deportment

Participate in a panel discussion as speaker, moderator, or evaluator. When participating in a panel discussion, remember the following points. III

1. Research the topic.
2. Plan some of the contributions you are to make.
3. Speak in an informal, conversational manner.
4. Speak in a strong, clear voice.
5. Don't let one person talk too much, and don't let long periods of silence occur.

Participate in a role-playing situation in which people are trying to achieve a specific purpose. One person obviously contributes to or detracts from the achievement of the group. III (SS 400)

WRITING SKILLS

LA 530 Show that you can use grammatical principles correctly in written material. III

Recognize general nouns and specific nouns. II

SECONDARY

Recognize action verbs and forms of the verb *to be.* II

Given a sentence with the verb in the passive voice, write the verb in the active voice. III

Given a sentence with a noun and its modifier(s) underlined, rewrite the sentence replacing the underlined words with a single noun that means the same thing but is more concise. III

Given a sentence with a verb and its modifier(s) underlined, rewrite the sentence replacing the underlined words with a single verb that has the same meaning. III

Recognize the following parts of speech in given sentences. II

1. Noun
2. Verb
3. Adjective
4. Adverb
5. Preposition
6. Conjunction
7. Pronoun
8. Interjection

Given selected sentences, recognize simple and complete subjects and predicates. II

Given selected sentences, recognize the following. II

1. Direct object (object complement)
2. Indirect object
3. Subject complement (predicate noun, predicate adjective)
4. Object of preposition
5. Appositive

Given selected sentences, recognize verbs in the active voice and verbs in the passive voice. II

Given selected sentences, recognize transitive and intransitive verbs. II

Recognize simple, compound, complex, and compound-complex sentences in written material. II

Recognize adjective clauses, adverb clauses, and noun clauses in written material. II

SECONDARY

Recognize participles, gerunds, and infinitives in written material. II

Write sentences using the following forms and label each verb as one of these forms: (1) verb transitive, (2) verb intransitive, and (3) linking verb. III

Write sentences that contain nouns used as each of the following: (1) subject, (2) direct object, (3) indirect object, (4) subject complement (predicate nominative), and (5) appositive. III

Write sentences using the comparative and superlative forms of the adverb and adjective, and label the adverbs and adjectives as comparative or superlative. III

Write several sentences that contain prepositional phrases and underline each prepositional phrase. III

Write sentences that contain each of the following kinds of phrases: (1) participial phrase, (2) gerund phrase, and (3) infinitive phrase. III

Write sentences using the following types of clauses: (1) independent clause, and (2) subordinate (dependent) clause. III

Write compound, complex, and compound-complex sentences. III

Write a paragraph in which you use correctly the following grammatical forms. Underline and identify each form that you use. III

1. Verb transitive
2. Verb intransitive
3. Linking verb
4. Subject
5. Direct object
6. Indirect object
7. Subject complement
8. Appositive
9. Comparative form of an adjective or adverb
10. Superlative form of an adjective or adverb
11. At least two prepositional phrases

Write a paragraph in which you use correctly the following kinds of sentences and the sentence elements listed below. Underline and identify each sentence element that you use. III

1. Compound sentence
2. Complex sentence
3. Compound-complex sentence, including a participial phrase, a gerund phrase, an infinitive phrase, an independent clause, and a subordinate (dependent) clause

Recognize errors in the use of pronouns, adjectives, adverbs, and verbs in written material. II

Recognize sentence fragments, run-on sentences, relationships between clauses, and parallel structure in written material. II

LA 525 Show your understanding of word uses in written material. II (LA 320)

Given a pair of homonyms, define each homonym. I

Given a list of words, recognize the words that are similar in meaning. II

Given a word, identify its antonym from a given list. I

Given an incomplete analogy and a list of words, recognize the word that completes the analogy. II

Given the first half of several different kinds of word analogies, recognize another pair of words that are analogous in the same way that the words in the first pair are. II

Recognize the difference in meaning between closely related words and give examples from personal observation to illustrate it. (Use a dictionary whenever necessary.) II

Given sentences each of which contains a malapropism (a word that sounds somewhat like the one intended), recognize the malapropism and replace it with the correct word. II

Present the meaning of common words in two of the following ways: a formal definition, a synonym, a definition by contrast, and/or a working definition. II

SECONDARY

LA 540 Show that you can recognize and use correct punctuation. III

Use correct punctuation and capitalization in written material. III

Write several sentences that use the comma in the following ways.
1. To separate items in a series
2. To separate independent clauses
3. To set off introductory subordinate clauses or long introductory phrases
4. To set off such nonessential elements as names used in direct address, appositives, nonrestrictive participial phrases and nonrestrictive clauses, and parenthetical expressions
5. To separate the items in dates and addresses

Write an example of a compound sentence correctly punctuated by a semicolon. Write a sentence that illustrates another use of the semicolon. III

Write two sentences, using the colon in a different way in each sentence. III

Use quotation marks in sentences. III (LA 670)

Write a paragraph in which you use correctly the following marks of punctuation. III
1. Comma
   a. To separate items in a series
   b. To set off independent clauses
   c. After introducing subordinate clauses or long introductory phrases
   d. To set off such nonessential elements as names used in direct address, appositives, nonrestrictive participial phrases and nonrestrictive clauses, and parenthetical expressions
   e. To separate the items in dates and addresses
2. Semicolon
3. Colon
4. Quotation marks
5. Parentheses

LA 545 Show that you can use various forms and techniques to demonstrate skill in expository writing. III (LA 605)

Summarize a given paragraph showing that you understand the main idea. III

SECONDARY

From a list of topics, recognize the topic that would be most suitable for development in a paragraph of about 150 words. II

Write a topic sentence suitable for development in a paragraph of about 150 words. The sentence should be a generalization, it should be logical, and it should make a commitment. III

Given a topic sentence, write at least four sentences to develop it, using the commitment-response technique. III

Write three paragraphs, one with coordinate sequence, one with subordinate sequence, and one with mixed sequence. III

Write three paragraphs using expressions that link sentences by signaling relationships between them. Underline the transitional expressions. III

Write a paragraph using details to develop the topic sentence. III

Write a paragraph using examples to develop the topic sentence. III

Write a paragraph using definitions to develop the topic sentence. III

Write a paragraph using comparisons to develop the topic sentence. III

Use facts and opinions to develop the topic sentence of a paragraph. III

From a topic sentence write a paragraph that presents a cause-effect relationship. III

For a paragraph write a closing sentence that strengthens and unifies the main impression of the paragraph and makes the reader feel that it is complete. III

Given statements about ideas, objects, or events, classify them as statements that identify the ideas, objects, or events and statements that define them. II

SECONDARY

Write a 300-word paper based on the definition of an idea, an object, or an event. III

Given a specific point of view from which to classify people or things, develop a scheme of classification that fulfills these requirements. V (SC 520)

1. There is only one principle applied at each stage of the classification.
2. The subclassifications under each classification account for all the members in the classification.

Write a 300-word paper that gives information about people or things according to a scheme of classification determined by a specific point of view. III (SC 520)

Given a class of people or things, recognize five or more specific individuals or things in that class. II (SC 520)

Write a 300-word paper that explains a class of people or things by using a specific member within the class to illustrate it. III

Identify three ways in which one person or thing can be compared with another person or thing. I

Write a 300-word paper in which you compare one person or thing with another person or thing. Before you begin your comparison, state (1) the particular way in which you will make your comparison, and (2) the pattern of organization you will use to make your comparison. VI

Given something to be analyzed, describe three ways in which it may be analyzed. II

In a written technical description, present a complete and systematic body of information about a given object for sale. III (MA 690)

Given the name of a particular organization or process, analyze in a 300-word paper the manner in which the parts of the organization or process work together. IV

Given an article and its summary, recognize whether the summary is a précis. II

Use the various elements of précis writing by reading a given literary selection and writing a short précis of it. III

After examining given factual material represented graphically, write a one-paragraph factual report summarizing the significant facts that this material presents. II

Paraphrase a poem or literary passage that deals with war. II

Write your definition of success in a 500-word essay that includes an introduction, a body, and a conclusion. The essay should also contain examples of persons who measure up to your definition. III (SS 690)

Recall something said or written that brought about a definite change in your behavior. Write a brief narrative of what happened to make you change, including the following points. III (SS 395)
1. Circumstances of your life at the time of the change
2. What it was that was said or written
3. How it was said or written
4. Who said or wrote it
5. What the change in your behavior was
6. How long the change lasted

LA 547 Show that you can prepare and present a written argument. III

Write a 200-word argument in which you state under what conditions, if any, you think war might be justified. III

Develop an argument of from 200 to 500 words on the affirmative or the negative side of a current issue. Use as many of the following suggestions for effective persuasion as are appropriate. V (LA 690)
1. Be modest in your claims; exaggeration, cocksureness, and bragging offend.
2. Appeal to such human motivations as the reader's desire for security, desire to be liked and appreciated, and desire to help others.
3. Choose words carefully.
4. Be honest and sincere.
5. End with a strong statement of the case.

SECONDARY

STUDY SKILLS

LA 550 Show your understanding of strategies for taking tests. II (SC 375)

Recognize strategies in preparing for test-taking. II

Identify factors influencing general test performance and ways of dealing with these factors. I

Use effective strategies for dealing with subjective (essay) test questions. III

Use effective strategies for dealing with objective (short answer) test questions. II

LA 555 Show your understanding of strategies involved in developing good study skills. II (SC 375)

Identify reasons for practicing good study skills. I

Identify ten major principles of learning. I

Identify ten study habits that should be kept in mind before you begin to work. I

Describe five study habits or skills that help you to overview reading materials. List four related principles of learning. II

Describe four study skills that help you to read with greater understanding and retention and relate these skills to principles of learning. II

Use the seven major study skills for listening. III (LA 505)

Recognize the principles for learning that relate to listening skills, and discuss rewards that can come with good listening. III (LA 505)

LA 557 Make judgments based on the evaluation of dictionaries. VI

Using Webster's *Third New International Dictionary* or *The American Heritage Dictionary* as your source, list at least twelve kinds of information given about word entries. I

Evaluate various entries in Webster's *Third New International Dictionary, The American Heritage Dictionary,* and a small desk dictionary in terms of the adequacy, recency, and extensiveness of the definitions, and decide which is appropriate for given purposes. VI

Evaluate the status labels of Webster's *Third New International Dictionary* and *The American Heritage Dictionary* and decide, supporting adequately with examples, whether the function of any of the status labels tends to be arbitrary. VI

LA 560 Show that you can use the research skills and resources needed for a research paper. III

Identify the reference book or books that could be used to find each of the numbered items. Make your selection from these reference books: *Readers' Guide to Periodical Literature,* historical atlas, atlas, almanac, dictionary, encyclopedia. I

1. Author of a magazine article
2. African colonies in 1914
3. Physical geography of Europe
4. United States population by states, 1790–1960
5. Magazine articles on elections
6. Brief biography of Thomas Jefferson
7. Political map of Europe in 1648
8. List of presidents of the United States

Use the *Readers' Guide to Periodical Literature* to find articles on a given subject or author. III

Find biographical information about prominent personalities. III

Use literary reference books to locate the following types of information. III

1. Author of a quotation
2. Literary work in which a quotation was used
3. Complete quotation, when only a part of it is known
4. A few famous lines by an author
5. Quotations by various authors on a given subject

SECONDARY

Use the card catalogue, *Readers' Guide to Periodical Literature,* and any other special indexes in your school or community library. III

Using acceptable form, prepare cards for a working bibliography and use the listings to construct a final bibliography. III

Given the title of a book, use the card catalogue in a library to find (1) the author, (2) the publisher, (3) the copyright date, (4) the subject, (5) the call number. III

LA 565 Demonstrate your ability to perceive differences in written presentations by analyzing various documents. IV (LA 695)

Analyze a one-page written document, inferring the probable point of view of the author, the intended audience, and the purpose of the document. IV

Classify the following documents as "primary" or "secondary": (1) newspaper article, (2) textbook describing Napoleon's Battle of Waterloo, (3) novel, (4) critique of a novel, (5) research proposal, and (6) letter to a friend.

Recognize the definition of each of the following terms and an example of each term. II (LA 547)

1. Bias
2. Data
3. Fact
4. Frame of reference
5. Generalization
6. Hypothesis
7. Interpretation
8. Internal criticism
9. Logical fallacy
10. Primary sources
11. Secondary sources

Differentiate between historical statements that are factual and those that are interpretive. IV

Given a historical hypothesis and data, differentiate between the data that support the hypothesis and the data that do not support it. IV

Given conflicting interpretations of a historical event, determine the facts or assumptions that created points of difference between the two interpretations. IV (SS *passim*)

LA 570 Demonstrate your ability to combine the necessary elements of research and organization by writing a research paper. IV

Select a topic for research that meets the following criteria. III
1. It is of interest to you as a researcher.
2. It is researchable from sources available to you.
3. It is sufficiently limited to allow scholarly consideration.

Write a research paper that meets all of the established rules on form and style. Your paper will include (1) a title page, (2) an introductory statement that explains and limits the topic, (3) conclusions drawn as a result of the research, and (4) a complete bibliography. III

Using correct footnote form, write a footnote for your paper for material found in books or magazines. III

Recognize and use the following abbreviations in written research. III

1. ibid.
2. loc. cit.
3. op. cit.
4. et al.
5. etc.
6. f. or ff.
7. p. or pp.
8. ed.
9. sic
10. vol. or vols.

PERSONAL COMMUNICATION AND DEVELOPMENT SKILLS

LA 575 Show your understanding of military obligations. II

Define the terms *draft, selective service,* and *conscription.* I

Identify the responsibilities of every 18-year-old male in connection with registering for the draft. I

Identify examples of the five groups (Class I-V) that local selective service boards use for classifying draft registrants and the main steps a registrant can take if he chooses to appeal his classification. I

Identify the way that draft registrants are selected for induction. I

SECONDARY

Compare the major alternatives open to men for fulfilling their military obligation: draft, enlistment, reserves, and commission. Evaluate the advantages and disadvantages of each alternative and suggest which alternative individuals in various circumstances should choose. VI (SS 575)

Design an alternative method of meeting the nation's defense manpower needs and compare it with the present selective service system. V

LA 580 Show that you can use information about various occupations, your interests, and your test scores to suggest first and second choices of long-range goals. III

Identify sources of information about specific job openings. I

Find information about a specific job or jobs you are interested in. III

Prepare and deliver an informative speech about job openings you are interested in. III

Recognize ways in which a person can provide information about himself when applying for (1) a job, (2) admission to college, and (3) admission to a training program. II

Complete a sample application form for (1) a job, (2) a college, or (3) a training program. II

Prepare a concise resume of your qualifications for a job, including the following kinds of information: (1) personal data, (2) educational background, (3) type of work desired or objective, (4) special skills or abilities, (5) work experience, and (6) references. III

Write an answer to one of seven possible essay questions that may be included on application forms. III

Role-play a person who is being interviewed for (1) a job, (2) admission to college, or (3) a training program. III

Evaluate the following as immediate post-high-school options, using job opportunity, personal interest, social restrictions, and personal goals as criteria for your evaluation. Decide which is the best immediate choice for you: (1) college, (2) training program, (3) work, (4) military service, or (5) marriage. VI

Discuss how the following adult roles can be coordinated to produce a life of self-fulfillment: (1) employee, (2) husband or wife, (3) mother or father, (4) student, and (5) citizen. III

Define the following terms: *university, college, junior college, public college, private college, religiously affiliated, nondenominational, coeducational, liberal arts,* and *accredited.* I

List several specific kinds of information you should obtain for each of these areas before choosing a college: (1) cost, (2) entrance requirements, (3) academic programs, and (4) college life. I

Describe the kinds of information you would expect to find from the following sources of information: (1) resource people, (2) college handbooks, (3) college catalogues, and (4) a visit to a college campus. II

List four main sources of funds required to meet the cost of a college education. I (MA 690)

Write a one- or two-page report on three colleges, including information on (1) cost, (2) entrance requirements, (3) academic programs, (4) college life, and (5) the advantages and disadvantages of each college for you. III

LA 585 Show that you can use logic and rhetoric to solve problems, to write and discuss material, and to present arguments or debates. III (LA 547)

Recognize the irrelevant statements in a given written passage. II

Given written passages in which the following rhetorical techniques are used, recognize each technique. II

SECONDARY

1. Progressive refinement of a core statement
2. High verb density
3. Linking and transitional expressions
4. Repetition of phrasal or clausal structure
5. Metaphor
6. Imagery
7. Relation of sentence pattern to content

Using inductive logic, support an argument for a given statement. III

Given two statements of a syllogism, write a third statement that completes the syllogism. III

Determine valid deductive arguments (syllogisms) and invalid ones. Identify the source(s) of the fallacies. IV

Given passages of argument, determine the main ideas and the patterns of logic (induction, deduction, analogy) that they contain and determine their logical validity. IV

Analyze given statements as judgments of fact, as inferences, or as value judgments. IV

Make inferences derived from a given paragraph. IV

Given a list of patterns for solving problems, suggest which patterns might be used to solve specified problems. II

Develop an essay on an assigned topic, using several rhetorical strategies and several patterns of logic. V

Given a list of propositions, determine whether they are arguable or nonarguable. IV

Given a list of arguable propositions, determine which ones are propositions of fact and which are propositions of action. IV

Given an arguable or major proposition, suggest at least five minor propositions or arguments to support it. II

Given evidence in support of an arguable proposition, determine which evidence is fact and which is opinion. IV

Given an arguable proposition, present a defense or refutation of the proposition arrived at through induction, deduction, and analogy. III

Given an arguable proposition, use the following criteria to develop a 400-word argument that supports or refutes it. IV

1. The major proposition of your argument has at least five relevant minor propositions to support it.
2. The evidence you use in support of your propositions really supports those propositions.
3. The reasoning in your argument is as strong as you can make it.

HISTORY AND DIALECTOLOGY

LA 590 Show that you can find and use information about changes that have occurred in the development of language. III

Given a list of twenty adjectives and nouns pertaining to a single area, explain the etymology of the words, explain how each is used today, and suggest how each might be used in the future. II

Given a list of fifteen words pertaining to the area of mood and feeling, explain the etymology of each word and give examples of its use today. II

Using references, represent on a time line the following invasions that effected changes in the English language: (1) Picts, (2) Danes, (3) Normans, (4) Anglo-Saxons and Jutes, and (5) Romans. III

Using references, represent on a time line the following events and influences that affected the English language. III

1. Modern British was spoken.
2. Germanic tribes invaded England (*Beowulf* written, place and date unknown).
3. Church in medieval England influenced language.
4. Norman French was used as the language of court and school.
5. Chaucer wrote in English (Middle English).
6. Printing was invented in Belgium.
7. Caxton's Flemish workers influenced English.
8. Renaissance humanism influenced English.
9. British Empire expanded and the English language changed (as in America).

SECONDARY

Describe, with specific examples, changes in the English language that indicate its popularization (the language of written English approximating the language and style of spoken English). II

Write a small dictionary of dialect and slang. Present entries in alphabetical order. Include (1) several examples, labeled dialect, slang, jargon, argot, and cant; (2) a clear definition for each entry (do not use the root of the word to define the entry, such as *groovy,* "the state of being in the groove"); (3) a context following each definition that shows how the world is being used; (4) a listing in the front of the dictionary that defines the meaning of your labels (dialect, slang, jargon, argot, and cant); and (5) a parts-of-speech label for each entry. III

Find and list British English terms and phrases equivalent to the following American English ones, checking for spelling, vocabulary, and pronunciation differences. III

1. humor
2. traveler
3. gas
4. theater
5. freight train
6. truck
7. wagon
8. grade crossing
9. ax
10. windshield
11. hood (of car)
12. catalogue
13. wrench
14. streetcar
15. medieval
16. movies
17. check (credit)
18. check (baggage)
19. castle
20. charm

Develop a research paper of 1000–3000 words on a limited aspect of the topic "Place Names in the United States." Consider using the names of states, counties, cities, towns, villages, or streets. Consider such influences as word origin, spelling and changes in spelling, pronunciation and changes in pronunciation, meanings, and exceptions to general trends in any of these areas. V

LA 595 Demonstrate your ability to perceive relationships in theories of language development. IV

In the following list of the major areas of linguistic specialization, match each of these terms with a statement that describes it accurately. I

1. Dialect study
2. Grammar
3. Descriptive linguistics
4. Language history
5. Usage
6. Lexicography
7. Semantics
8. Psycholinguistics

Describe three major theories about the origin of language. Select the theory you favor and explain your opinion. II

After examining both sides of the controversy, explain whether you think it is the lexicographer's responsibility to *prescribe* language or to *describe* language. Give four supportive reasons for your conclusion, citing at least three sources. II

Apply the idea that man may be judged by his language to examples from current speech and writing. III

Describe the following theories of the origin of language: (1) dingdong, (2) Bow-wow, and (3) Pooh-Pooh. II

LA 600 Demonstrate your ability to perceive the relationship of emotional and psychological impact of words to semantics. IV

Given two or more words having the same primary meaning (denotation), suggest an implied or secondary meaning (connotation) for each word. II

Given a word that is neutral in association, suggest two synonymous words or phrases, one that is favorable in association and one that is unfavorable. II

Rewrite a given passage, replacing selected terms with more specific terms that fit the context of the passage. II

Classify sentences and passages as colloquial, uneducated, or formal expression. II

Given a list of figurative expressions, recognize the expressions that give a fresh interpretation of human experience. II

Given a passage including unnecessary words and phrases, rewrite it in the most condensed and economical form possible. II

Match each of the following terms related to the study of semantics with a statement that identifies it accurately. I

SECONDARY

1. Referment
2. Verbal
3. Nonverbal
4. Semantically safe
5. Verifiable
6. Emotive
7. Subjective
8. Objective
9. Affective
10. Analogy
11. Generalization
12. Inference
13. Logic
14. Levels of abstraction
15. Value judgment
16. Color words
17. Propaganda
18. Literacy
19. Denotation
20. Connotation
21. Communication

Evaluate written statements as to whether or not their words are at a level of abstraction too high to communicate a clear message. VI

Given the picture of a particular event and a statement that is a value judgment of the event, rewrite the statement so that it expresses only what is semantically safe to express. III

Recognize written examples of each of the following semantic fallacies: (1) unverifiable referent, (2) false analogy, (3) color words, (4) overgeneralization, (5) confusing facts with inference, and (6) confusing facts with value judgment. II

CLASSIFICATION, INTERPRETATION, AND ANALYSIS OF LITERARY FORMS

LA 605 Show your understanding of literary terms and devices by recognizing them in the short story, the novel, drama, biography, and poetry. II

Describe the setting of a short story. II

Recognize examples of repetition in a piece of literature and explain why they are used. II (LA 585)

Recognize examples of foreshadowing in a piece of literature and explain their use. II (LA 675)

Recognize literary symbols and explain their symbolic meaning. II (LA 675)

Given one or more figures of speech that interpret a particular human experience, recognize the experience interpreted. II (LA 675)

Given a passage that has a specific tone, explain what the tone of the passage tells about the author's attitude toward his subject. II (LA 665)

Recognize an example of irony either from your reading or from everyday life and explain why it is ironic. II

Given several ironic statements in their context, classify them as lighthearted, fun-poking, thought-provoking, or vicious. II (LA 665)

Recognize rhyme scheme by scanning several lines of poetry. II

Use letter patterns to describe the rhyme scheme of a poem. II

Recognize the metric pattern called iambic pentameter. II

Identify the characteristics of a poem written in blank verse. I

Identify the characteristics of a poem written in free verse. I

Recognize examples of alliteration in poetry. II

Explain the difference between simile and metaphor. II

Recognize the use of personification in poetry. II

Recognize the literal and figurative meaning of a symbol. II

Differentiate between the connotative and denotative meaning of words used by poets. IV (LA 600)

LA 610 Make a judgment involving the evaluation of a preference for a literary genre. Use the characteristics of each genre as criteria for your selection. VI

Identify the definition of prose and the definition of poetry. I

SECONDARY

Given a piece of writing, classify it as fiction or nonfiction. II

Identify two characteristics of each of the following types of prose: (1) novel, (2) short story, (3) drama, (4) biography, (5) autobiography, (6) essay. I

Identify two characteristics of each of the following types of poetry. I

1. Lyric	4. Ode	7. Epic
2. Elegy	5. Ballad	8. Pastoral
3. Sonnet	6. Dramatic	9. Narrative

Given a number of prose stories, recognize examples of a parable and a fable. II

Describe the kinds of love found in novels, short stories, plays, and poems you have read. II (SS 395)

List five characteristics of romanticism in literature and locate an example of each in your reading. I

Given selections of poetry, differentiate between those expressing sentiment and those expressing sentimentality. III

Prepare and present a short report, oral or written, on the content of a biography. Include these basic facts of the author's life: (1) when and where he was born, (2) how long he lived, and (3) what other books he wrote. III

Prepare and present a short report, oral or written, on the content of an autobiography. III

List three functions of myths in the ancient world. I

Identify twenty gods or other characters important in Greek mythology and identify each by a brief description. Also give the Roman name if one exists. I

Suggest an example of a myth that explains the origin of some natural phenomenon. II

Tell the story of one pair of lovers famous in Greek mythology. I

Tell the story of one of the great heroes of ancient Greece or Rome. I

Identify the origin of the following concepts: drama, tragedy, and comedy. I

Explain the influence of religion on early Greek drama. II

Identify the roles played by the characters in early Greek drama. I

Describe the physical elements of the Greek play. II

Determine at least three characteristics of *The Tragical History of Doctor Faustus* that make this drama a tragedy. IV

Given a play, such as *Oedipus Rex,* suggest five reasons why it could be considered a tragedy. II

Given a novel dealing with a modern hero, suggest at least three reasons why it could be considered tragic. II

Explain the influence that politics had on early Elizabethan drama. II

Describe the physical elements of the Elizabethan theater. II

Describe influences affecting modern drama. II

Describe the physical elements of the modern theater. II

Describe the similarities and differences between a Greek play, an Elizabethan play, and a modern play. II

LA 615 Demonstrate your ability to perceive relationships in the major works of an American poet. IV

Write ten or fifteen paragraphs about a major American poet. Each paragraph should cover a different aspect of his or her life. III

Present an oral reading of two poems written by a major American poet. III

SECONDARY

Explain the contextual meaning of given excerpts from poems by an American poet. II

Evaluate the relevance to your present-day world of given significant passages from a poem. VI

LA 620 Demonstrate your ability to perceive the techniques that Shakespeare employed in comedy and tragedy, and then distinguish the major characteristics of both types of drama. IV

Find information about (1) the political career of Julius Caesar, (2) Roman life and politics in the days of Julius Caesar, (3) Elizabethan drama, and (4) the Globe Theater that is necessary for an understanding of *Julius Caesar.* Find basic information about Shakespeare's life (not including exact dates). III

Summarize the plot of Shakespeare's *Julius Caesar.* II

Describe four important personality traits of each of the main characters in *Julius Caesar* (Brutus, Cassius, Antony, and Caesar) and explain, by referring to the text of the play, why you believe that the characters have these traits. II

Recognize six characteristics of Shakespearean tragedy in *Julius Caesar* and find a specific example of each. I

Discuss in writing one of the principal problems presented in *Julius Caesar.* These include the problems of loyalty, communication, governmental power, insurrection, idealism, martyrdom, and ambition. III

List six characteristics of Shakespearean comedy found in a play of your choice and give a specific example of each. I

Describe a Shakespearean tragic hero and a Greek tragic hero, citing at least three similarities and three differences. II

Analyze your observations and reading, citing three or four examples that show how the comic very often borders on the tragic. IV

Discuss the differences between comedy and tragedy and determine how Shakespeare elicited appropriate emotional responses from his audience. III (LA 600)

Write a scene of your own using the following techniques of effective drama: (1) soliloquy, (2) aside, (3) dialogue and visual clues that set the scene, (4) articulation of scenes (purpose of each scene in relation to the entire play), and (5) suspense. Be able to explain how you used each technique. V (LA 670)

LA 625 Demonstrate your ability to perceive components and relationships in essays, using techniques of literary criticism. IV

After reading an essay, infer the author's purpose (his central idea) and evaluate his skill in stimulating a response from the reader. Then analyze your reaction to his ideas. VI

After reading an essay, analyze its structure (the means the author uses to achieve his purpose), considering these points. IV

1. What are the main divisions of the essay and their relation to each other?
2. How long and how complex are the paragraphs and what is their relation to the main point?
3. How formal or informal is his language and his approach to his reader?

Write a one-page essay describing situations in which you are in a minority and situations in which you are in a majority. V

Analyze your emotional response to a short story or essay, listing the words, phrases, expressions, and passages that particularly appeal to the reader's senses. Then describe orally the emotional response, such as anger or disgust, that they stirred. IV (LA 600)

LA 630 Demonstrate your ability to perceive components and relationships in short stories, using techniques of literary criticism. IV

Recognize the theme (or main idea) of a short story and relate it to a situation with which you are familiar. II

Given a short story to read, describe its setting and explain why the setting is important to the story. II

Given a short story and statements about the story, recognize the statement that best describes its conflict and the statement that best describes its climax. II

SECONDARY

Analyze a short story to determine the point of view from which it is told. IV

Analyze a short story to determine the author's attitude toward the main character. IV

Analyze three ideas you received from reading a short story. Indicate which idea you think is the most important and which idea you think the author considers the most important. IV

Given a list of possible story plots, suggest possibilities for their development. II

Given a list of possible story plots and a list of several characters, suggest the characters who might be appropriately included in the development of the plot. II

Write an original short story that includes all of the major components (plot, character, point of view, tone, setting, and theme) and be able to explain how you used them in your story. V (LA 680)

Summarize the main events of a science-fiction story you have read. II

Interpret allusions made in the course of a science fiction story or novel. II

Discuss a philosophical or ethical point raised in a science fiction story or novel. III

Given a short story, determine the author's attitude toward his subject, characters, and situation. Identify the clues that led to your conclusion. IV

LA 635 Demonstrate your ability to perceive components and relationships in novels, using techniques of literary criticism and interpretation. IV

After reading a novel, summarize the important incidents in the plot and recognize the climax. II

Describe the following elements of a given novel: (1) plot, (2) setting, (3) point of view, and (4) characterization. II

Discuss a life situation described in a book you have read. III

Determine the setting of a novel and its effect on the characters and the plot. IV

Explain whether a novel contains examples of foreshadowing. Recognize and list any examples it contains. II

Determine whether or not a novel contains symbolism and interpret any examples it contains. IV

Write a paper explaining how the main events in a book support the theme and give examples of the author's main technique for building the climax (i.e., suspense, action, character analysis, conflict). II

Explain how an author uses techniques of short-story writing to create an effective novel. II

Analyze the importance of the arrangement of events in a novel by listing the events in the order in which the author placed them and then rearranging the order of those you consider key scenes. Evaluate the effect of the rearrangement on the novel as a whole, on the characters and their development, and on the reader. IV (LA 665)

After listing the main incidents in a novel, select one and write an alternate incident that the author might have chosen to illustrate his point. Evaluate the effectiveness of the change on the novel as a whole. VI (LA 680)

Write a different ending for the novel you have chosen, keeping in mind the nature of the characters involved and the pattern of events leading to the ending. Evaluate the effects of both the author's ending and yours. VI (LA 665)

Recognize the central theme in a novel and explain how the story illustrates it. II

SECONDARY

Discuss the central theme in a novel, considering how the novel illustrates it, and how the author might apply it to a contemporary situation. III

Given a work of science fiction you have read that deals with techniques of mind control, recognize the techniques that influence the behavior of the main character. II (SS 535)

Given two works of science fiction—one that pictures the future world as a Utopia and the other that gives an opposite impression—discuss how each deals with the following elements: (1) freedom of the individual, (2) the family unit, (3) education, (4) government, (5) work, and (6) leisure time. III (SS 535, SS 625)

Write a dictionary of vocabulary terms specific to a science-fiction novel such as *Out of the Silent Planet.* Give the word, its plural (if possible), and its meaning and tell what part of speech it is. III

LA 640 Demonstrate your ability to perceive components and relationships in character motivation and action. IV (SS 400)

Describe orally or in writing the physical appearance and personality of the three most important characters in a specific novel. II

Given a list of words that describe personality characteristics, match these with characters from some stories you have read. I

Given a list of specific characters from your reading, match them with a list of possible descriptions of these characters. I

Describe the characteristics and motives of characters in a short story. II

Describe the main character of a short story and tell which of his or her traits the author emphasizes. Give three examples from the story that show different ways of revealing character. II

Analyze the similarities between the thoughts and feelings of the main character in a short story and someone you know. (This "someone" may be you.) IV

SECONDARY

Write a paragraph describing an action for each of the following types of characters from short stories, novels, and plays you have read: (1) two characters whose actions are entirely responsible, (2) two whose actions are responsible in some respects, and (3) two whose actions are entirely irresponsible. Explain why your examples are valid. III

Analyze a play or novel with a comic hero (such as *Man of La Mancha* with Don Quixote or *Henry IV,* Part I, with Falstaff) to locate examples that show both comic and philosophic insights about human nature. IV

After reading a play or novel with a comic hero in it, recognize by name and example at least four of the devices the author uses to produce a comic effect. II

Given a list of literary works about heroic adventures, recognize the obstacles the hero must face and the specific qualities of heroism he reveals in meeting each obstacle. II

Given a character of heroic proportions, evaluate whether or not he is realistically presented by the author. Use a given definition of heroic characteristics as your criteria. VI

Analyze the tragedies surrounding three contemporary world figures whose careers have had a tragic end. Cite examples of how poor judgment and/or qualities in each individual's character caused his tragedy. IV (SS 695)

Given a character from a novel, a short story, or a play that you have read, decide whether a decision made by the character is ethically wrong or ethically right, and describe the consequences of his decision. VI

Given decisions of main characters in Puritan literature that you have read, recognize the elements of Puritanism in their decisions. II (SS 695)

Given a decision made by a character from a short story, a play, or a novel that you have read, recognize from the following list the way the character made the decision: (1) by himself, (2) through the influence of another person, (3) through circumstance, or (4) through two or more of these influences. Explain whether this way is consistent with what is known about the character. II

SECONDARY

Write a two-paragraph description for each of two characters who react differently to failure: one who is strengthened by failure and one who is weakened by failure. III

Given characters from novels, short stories, or plays that you have read, discuss them as follows. II
1. Describe the type of love that exists between two characters.
2. Describe how the love operates.
3. Describe the final consequences for the lover and for the recipient of the love.
4. Measure the love against your ideal standards of loving and receiving love.

Given characters from novels, short stories, and plays that you have read, analyze the growth and development of love (1) between one individual and another individual, (2) within the family, and (3) among people in general. IV

Analyze short stories, giving examples of characters who demonstrate the quality of sensitivity or compassion and of characters who communicate an indifference or lack of awareness of others' feelings. State specifically the clues in each case that enabled you to make the differentiation. IV

From among the works of such authors as Tennessee Williams, Ernest Hemingway, Carson McCullers, J. D. Salinger, and John Steinbeck, describe two characters who exemplify the following definition of an alienated individual: "an alienated individual is one who feels separated from an individual, a group, or a society." Explain why you regard the characters as alienated individuals. II

Using the following categories, determine the factor(s) in a given novel, short story, or poem that caused a character's alienation. IV
1. His own character makeup
2. How others treat him
3. Conditions in general

Given alienated characters from novels, short stories, and plays, predict in writing a course their lives might take if they are able to overcome their feeling of alienation. III

Write a paper of at least 500 words on one of the following subjects. V (LA 545)
1. Reasons for alienation
2. Consequences of alienation
3. Solutions for the problem of alienation

Describe the motivations and characteristics of various characters of a science-fiction novel. II

LA 645 Demonstrate your ability to perceive components and relationships in central conflicts between characters and/or ideas. IV

Given two passages that describe a situation of conflict, recognize the passage that shows you the situation rather than tells you about it. II

Explain the difference between internal and external conflict and give specific examples of each. II

Write one or two paragraphs about conflict between one individual and any institution and/or a group of people and any institution. III

Given situations of human group behavior in which one or more of the following types of conflicts occur, state the probable consequences of the conflict and propose alternate solutions to remove the conflict. Then, after evaluating the plans, decide which one would provide the most appropriate solution. VI (SS 500)
1. Conflicts about group goals
2. Conflicts about role behavior (differences in role expectations)
3. Conflicts about group norms

Design an original presentation—oral, visual, or written—about any one or a combination of the following. V
1. A person in conflict with himself
2. A person in conflict with another person
3. A person in conflict with several people
4. A group in conflict with another group
5. A nation in conflict with another nation

Given the following examples involving conflict between mores and laws, recognize reasons for the conflict: (1) 18th Amendment, (2) women's rights, and (3) religion and education. II (SS 545)

SECONDARY

After watching a TV drama involving social conflict, analyze the ways in which social or group pressure affects the behavior of characters in the play. IV

Given examples of conflict between an individual and the group he belongs to and a list of characters from stories you have read, predict possible reactions of specific characters to different conflict situations. III

Given examples of conflict between groups and a list of characters from stories you have read, predict possible reactions of specific characters to different conflict situations. III

Given a list of ways to solve conflict, select the solutions that might be used effectively in at least three conflicts from your reading. II

Write a 150- or 200-word descriptive passage that shows a boy, a girl, a man, or a woman in a situation of conflict. III

LA 650 Demonstrate your ability to combine concepts, principles, and generalizations by developing your own definition of culture and civilization based on literature that presents an anthropological view of man. V (SS 500, SS 545, SS 550)

Given characters in novels and plays about human society that you have read, evaluate their general behavior as consistent or as inconsistent with the following definition of *civilized behavior:* "Civilized behavior is the extent of concern one's actions show for the welfare of other people." In a sentence or two explain your evaluation of the behavior of each character. VI

Given a literary work that deals with people in a particular society, recognize in the makings of that society examples of the following elements: (1) political elements, (2) economic elements, (3) educational elements, (4) leisure time or avocational elements, (5) social elements, and (6) spiritual or religious elements. For example, a competitive grading system is an educational element in our civilization; the stock market and the graduated income tax are economic elements. II

Having classified elements in the makeup of a particular society described in novels and plays that you have read, determine those that encourage civilized behavior, those that both encourage and discourage civilized behavior, and those that discourage civilized behavior. As a guide, use the following definition of *civilized behavior:* "Civilized behavior is the extent of concern a person's actions show for the welfare of other people." III

Read a literary work about persons of another culture and describe five of their cultural attitudes, practices, or customs. Then explain why these attitudes, practices, or customs exist. Cite the source for your examples. II

Demonstrate that people of various cultures often express identical emotions. A set of pictures forming a collage, a set of film clips, or a set of audio tape sequences would be an appropriate demonstration. III

Describe at least six instances in which practices disapproved of by one culture are acceptable in another culture. Cite your sources. II

Recognize some attitudes, stereotypes, or biases about people of another cultural, racial, or ethnic group. Be able to cite examples from movies, literature, or personal experience that reinforce or modify the attitude, stereotype, or bias. II (SS 425)

Discuss the ideas and the mores that formed the background of today's generation of parents. Cite specific examples from all media of the 1930s and 1940s. III (SS 405)

Discuss the culture, the philosophy, and the essence of the society that is being created by tomorrow's generation of parents. Cite specific examples of all media from the 1960s. III (SS 256)

LA 655 Demonstrate your ability to perceive the relationship of literary contributions of black writers to development of an understanding of the historical and contemporary problems of black Americans. IV (SS 500, SS 525)

Recognize three distinct evolutionary periods in Malcolm X's life; then give at least one example of awareness or insight that Malcolm X gained in each period. II

Recognize at least three examples from *The Autobiography of Malcolm X* that illustrate why Malcolm X felt the black man has been robbed of his identity in America. II

Describe Malcolm X's account of his childhood experiences and those of an individual from a different minority group living in

America. List similarities and differences in their childhood experiences. II

Write a paper or produce a tape, developing an incident or a quotation from *The Autobiography of Malcolm X* that you found relevant to you or to your society. V

In a two-page essay, compare and contrast the ideas of Martin Luther King, Jr., and Malcolm X on the best hope for black-white relations in the American society. VI

Describe the American Negro's problem of double identity and explain how at least one black writer has dealt with it. II

Find five examples from poetry or prose by black writers that clearly negate the concept of the Negro as a stereotype. III

From black poetry of your selection, recognize at least three universal themes dealt with that are common to human experience (such as love, grief, and search for self) and describe how the poet individualizes the theme in his poem. II

From literature and from other forms of artistic expression (art, music, etc.), find and describe examples that illustrate at least five aspects of Negro culture that are distinctive (uniquely black). II

From your reading and from other observations (photos, television, films, records), suggest at least four specific examples of how blacks have used the weapons of humor or creativity against racialism and indifference. II

Describe five basic causes of racial disorders, using a published report such as the Kerner Report and citing your source. III

LA 660 Demonstrate your ability to perceive the relationship of intellectual and social implications in literature. IV

Given stories, novels, and plays about young people with a growing awareness of what it means to be an adult, (1) recognize the elements of the adult world of which young people are becoming aware, (2) describe the events that produce this growing awareness, and (3) describe the reactions of young people to their growing awareness. II

SECONDARY

Given a list of literary works about young people, suggest examples for each of the following kinds of relationships that exist between characters in the literary works. II
1. An adult helps a young person grow up.
2. An adult helps a young person grow up in some respects and hinders him in others.
3. An adult hinders a young person from growing up.

Based on your observations of conformity in novels, short stories, plays, and life, write an extended definition of the term *conformity.* III

Given novels, short stories, and plays that you have read, recognize areas in which the major character did or did not conform to existing social standards at the time depicted. II

Describe the consequences of the nonconformity of a given literary character who is a nonconformist. II

Analyze poems or songs to locate examples of man's sensitivity or indifference to his fellows or to his environment. IV

Demonstrate man's sensitivity to people and to his environment with cartoons, photographs, or pictures and with newspaper or magazine clippings. III

Discuss social values and evils that cause corruption or make some people victims of their society. III

Recognize definitions of each of the following terms often used in reference to minority groups and recognize one example of each of these terms: (1) prejudice, (2) stereotype, (3) discrimination, (4) bigotry, (5) racism, and (6) intolerance. II

Given a list of statements describing group relationships, recognize the statements that show prejudice and those that do not. II

Given a list of prejudicial statements, infer the basis of the author's prejudices in each case: (1) fear, (2) greed, or (3) ignorance. II

Given descriptions of particular products that result from applied technology, determine which one of the following categories each product belongs to. Write an essay supporting each classification you make. III

1. Products that may enhance the quality of our lives directly
2. Products that may enhance the quality of our lives indirectly (by freeing us for other pursuits, for example)
3. Products that merely add to the quantity of things heaped up for our use and abuse

Evaluate the extent to which the principal character of a given novel or play that you have read succeeded in achieving the "American dream." (The "American dream" is the belief that any man can raise himself by his bootstraps to become what he wishes to be and to attain what he wishes to have.) VI

Develop a five-year program whereby a 16-year-old boy or girl living in an underprivileged area can find ample opportunity to acquire the skills necessary for a productive life in the United States. Before you put your program in final form, clearly define the terms *underprivileged area* and *productive life* and do the research necessary for the development of such a program. V (SS 550)

Given a selection from a list of literary works dealing with social injustice, recognize attitudes held by characters in those works that either cause or reinforce unjust social conditions. II (SS 695)

From articles, essays, and poems, infer meanings that are given to human freedom by the author. II

Having read a short story, a novel, or a play that deals with the subject of war, describe two attitudes toward war that are revealed by the thoughts, speech, and/or actions of two characters. II

Paraphrase a poem or literary passage that deals with war. II

original writing

LA 665 Show your understanding of style differences in written material. II

Given two sentences that describe the same person, recognize the sentence that focuses your attention on the person described rather than on the person who wrote the sentence. II

Write a description of a person, using nouns and verbs that show the person described rather than merely tell about the person. III

Given two passages that describe the same location, recognize the passage that contains nouns and verbs that show the reader the location rather than merely tell the reader about it. II

LA 670 Show that you can use dialogue to develop characterization. III

Write a two-page dialogue between two persons who hold opposing views on (1) American involvement in Vietnam, or (2) American assistance to Israel in the Arab-Israeli war. III

Write a 150-word dialogue that shows four or more of the following things about each person in the dialogue: (1) age, (2) sex, (3) occupation, (4) interests, (5) temperament, and (6) outlook. III

LA 675 Show that you can use special techniques in descriptive writing. III

Given a list of descriptive words and phrases, explain which would be effective in expressing specific emotions. II

Given two passages that describe a tragic event, recognize the passage that understates the event. II

Write a 150-word descriptive passage about a tragic event using understatement. III

Given two passages that describe a situation of conflict, recognize the passage that shows you the situation rather than tells you about it. II

Write several passages that describe situations of conflict, maintaining a verb density of 1:6 or higher. III

Write a 150- or 200-word descriptive passage that shows a boy, a girl, a man, or a woman in a situation of conflict. III

Write a two-paragraph description for each of two characters who react differently to failure: one who is strengthened by failure, and one who is weakened by failure. III

SECONDARY

Write a 150-word descriptive passage (location, person, event) in which the specific tone you give to the passage clearly indicates your attitude toward your subject. III

Write a 150- or 200-word descriptive passage that creates a mood of expectancy through appropriate choice of words and appropriate length of sentences. III

Write a paper in which you describe a person who communicates effectively. III

LA 680 Using the techniques of creative writing, demonstrate your ability to combine concepts, principles, and generalizations by writing original compositions. V

Relate two different things, such as a doorbell and a rattlesnake, by writing a paragraph in which you make connections between ideas. V

Write a paragraph in which you as the author assume the role of a thing, animate or inanimate, that is completely different from your own personal experiences. For instance, write a paragraph describing yourself as a zero—see the world as a zero might see it. V

Use two words to sum up conflicting natures of an object or idea in a compressed conflict. Then write a short paragraph justifying the meaning of your compressed conflict. For example, a compressed conflict describing a fire might be "life-saving destroyer." III

After viewing a picture from a magazine or newspaper, write a fictitious newspaper story about what is happening in the picture. III

Write two extended metaphors of approximately 100 words, one interpreting the experience of winning and the other interpreting the experience of losing. V

Given a particular human experience, write an extended metaphor of about 150 words interpreting that experience. V

Write a piece of prose that contains both narration and description. V

Write a piece of prose that contains both exposition and argument. V

Given a written passage whose tone makes us judge a character's action unfavorably, rewrite the passage and change the tone so that we judge the same character's actions favorably (or vice versa). III

Write a skit or dialogue portraying a comic character from literature, the theatre, television, or your own imagination in an incongruous or humorous setting. (For example, portray Don Quixote in a computerized classroom.) V

Write a story that shows a young person growing up in a particular location with an increasing awareness of what it means to be an adult in that location. V

Write a scene of your own, using the techniques of effective drama: (1) soliloquy, (2) aside, (3) dialogue and visual clues that set the scene, (4) articulation of scenes (purpose of each scene in relation to the entire play), and (5) suspense. Be able to explain how you used each technique. V

Given three class periods devoted to creative writing, write at least two pieces of prose or poetry. V

Write an original short story that includes plot, character, point of view, tone, setting, and theme. Be able to explain how you used them in your story. V

Oral and Dramatic Interpretation

LA 685 Show that you can present oral interpretations. III

Practice and present a five-minute reading of a prose selection. Your reading will be judged on (1) volume, (2) rate, (3) pitch, (4) gestures, (5) body movements, and (6) mood changes. III

Present a reading of three poems either written by the same person or related in theme. To accompany the presentation, you must provide an introduction and transitional remarks. III

Present to the class an excerpt of dialogue between two people in a play. Use a different voice to represent each character. III

Present an oral reading of two poems of your choice by the same author. III (LA 615)

Present an oral reading of a scene from *Julius Caesar* and give examples from that scene of at least six of the following: (1) puns, (2) blank verse, (3) prose speeches, (4) run-on lines, (5) end-stopped lines, (6) rhyming couplets, (7) repetition, (8) metaphors, (9) similes. III

critical analysis of media

LA 690 Show that you can use the techniques of mass media for persuading an audience. III

Given examples of common propaganda devices, classify them as being associated with (1) name-calling, (2) glittering generalities, (3) transfer, (4) testimonial, (5) plain folks, (6) card-stacking, and (7) band wagon. II (SS 425)

Given examples of common propaganda appeals, classify them as being associated with (1) survival, (2) safety, (3) belonging, (4) prestige, or (5) fulfillment. II

Having identified the primary motive of a particular propagandist, classify the motive as showing (1) little concern other than for his or his group's welfare, (2) about as much concern for others as for his or his group's welfare, or (3) more concern for others than for his or his group's welfare. Give a brief explanation for your classification. II

Given the name and a brief description of a past propaganda campaign, find additional information about the campaign so that you may (1) describe one direct consequence of the campaign, and (2) describe two indirect consequences of the campaign. You must support the validity of the direct consequence you list by identifying the source of your information. Furthermore, you must list at least two different sources of information. For the indirect consequences, use your imagination. III (SS 580)

Develop a propaganda campaign for or against an idea or action. Your piece of propaganda must make use of at least one of the common propaganda devices and at least one of the common propaganda appeals. V

Discuss the possibility that social values in America are controlled or at least manipulated by TV producers and advertisers. Cite examples to illustrate your points. III

Recognize ploys and devices used by automobile salesmen in selling automobiles. II

With examples from newspapers and magazines illustrate the techniques used by advertisers to create favorable attitudes toward their product and to persuade customers to buy. II

Explain each of the following techniques used by film makers and relate each to the process of communication: (1) framing, (2) long long-shot, (3) long-shot, (4) medium shot, (5) close close-up, (6) close-up, (7) motion, (8) camera position (angle), (9) facial features, (10) background, (11) contrasts, (12) editing, (13) montage, (14) lighting, (15) color, (16) music, (17) sound effects, (18) commentary, (19) dialogue. II

LA 695 Make judgments about media by evaluating different presentations. VI

After viewing selected photographs and/or listening to records or tapes of dramatic scenes, analyze any reactions you experienced by listing ideas or sensations that led to your response. IV

Given a particular event, determine some of the causes and effects of the event and express your findings in a 300-word paper. IV

Demonstrate how people display opposite emotions about the same event with at least three examples from pictures in newspapers or magazines. III

SECONDARY

In writing and/or discussion, analyze both written and oral presentations to locate faulty generalizations. IV

Given a reading selection containing a theme supported by facts, determine the accuracy of supporting details by consulting appropriate special references. III

Analyze a news story as reported in two different publications, broadcasts, or telecasts to locate examples of bias or misleading use of facts revealed by the way the various news media dealt with the same story. IV

Analyze a statement made for the mass media to determine the author's attitude toward minority groups and equal opportunity. IV

After watching a TV drama involving social conflict, determine how social or group pressure affects the behavior of characters in the play. IV

After viewing four or five TV programs for two or three weeks, evaluate them by producing a TV guide that indicates (1) the nature of each program, (2) the audience for whom it is intended, and (3) your critique of the program. VI

Summarize ways in which the consumer can avoid signing fraudulent contracts and can prevent himself from being legally bound to exorbitant, long-term financial agreements. II (MA 690)

Analyze a personal reaction to a movie involving a strong bond of sympathy for one of the major characters. Label the strongest emotion you felt as you identified with the character and analyze the technique used by the director to obtain that reaction from you. IV

Suggest films that are appropriate for showing the high school students in a film-study course. Explain your choice of films. II

In a working group, produce a brief film of one of the following. V
1. A commercial or a parody of a commercial
2. A documentary on a current topic
3. An art film
4. A narrative film with a serious theme

TERMINAL OBJECTIVES

TERMINAL OBJECTIVES

LISTENING SKILLS

PRIMARY

LA 005 Show that you can follow oral directions. III

LA 010 Show that you can differentiate between sounds. III

LA 015 Show that you can remember information from an oral presentation. I

INTERMEDIATE

LA 200 Show your understanding of information presented orally by summarizing and interpreting the content. II

LA 205 Make a judgment on techniques used by the speaker in an oral presentation. VI

SECONDARY

LA 505 Demonstrate your ability to perceive content and speech techniques by listening to oral presentations. IV

SPEAKING SKILLS

PRIMARY

LA 020 Show that you can present ideas orally. III

LA 025 Show that you can present descriptions of personal experiences. III

LA 030 Show that you can present ideas effectively to an audience. III

LA 035 Show that you can participate in group discussions. III

INTERMEDIATE

LA 210 Show that you can plan and conduct personal interviews. III

TERMINAL OBJECTIVES

LA 215 Show that you can make informal oral presentations. III

LA 220 Show that you can use techniques for preparing an organized oral report. III

LA 225 Show that you can present an organized oral report. III

LA 230 Show that you can participate in achieving the goals of a discussion group. III

LA 235 Show that you can apply techniques for leading a discussion. III

SECONDARY

LA 510 Show that you can prepare a speech using techniques appropriate to your purpose as a speaker. III

LA 515 Show that you can use the speech forms and techniques appropriate to your purpose as a speaker. III

LA 520 Show that you can present a speech or another form of oral presentation using the appropriate techniques. III

LA 525 Show that you can participate in group situations in which personal opinions and values are being expressed. III

reading skills

PRIMARY

LA 040 Show your understanding of relationships by classifying objects according to size, shape, and number. II

LA 045 Show that you know how to follow a left-to-right sequence. I

LA 050 Show that you know the letters of the alphabet. I

TERMINAL OBJECTIVES

LA 055 Show your understanding of the similarities and differences among sounds. II

LA 060 Show your understanding of similarities and differences among visual symbols. II

LA 065 Show that you can apply a sound to its written symbol to read new words. III

LA 070 Show that you can use the analysis of word structure to read new words. III

LA 075 Show that you can recognize and use given aspects of words. III

LA 080 Show your understanding of word forms and sentence patterns by reading orally. II

LA 085 Show that you can follow written directions. III

LA 090 Show that you can apply various techniques for reading new words independently. III

INTERMEDIATE

LA 240 Show your understanding of the meaning of words and phrases by relating them to contextual uses. II

LA 245 Show that you can use structural analysis to recognize and use the correct forms of words. III

LA 250 Show that you can apply skills of phonetic and structural analysis to improve your spelling and reading. III

WRITING SKILLS

PRIMARY

LA 095 Show that you can make visually distinct patterns. III

TERMINAL OBJECTIVES

LA 100 Show that you know the letters of the alphabet. I

LA 105 Show that you can communicate thoughts in complete sentences. III

INTERMEDIATE

LA 255 Show that you can prepare and present ideas in logical form and sequence. III

LA 260 Demonstrate your ability to combine concepts, principles, and generalizations by organizing sentences and paragraphs to develop a topic. V

SECONDARY

LA 530 Show that you can use grammatical principles correctly in written material. III

LA 535 Show your understanding of word uses in written material. II

LA 540 Show that you can recognize and use correct punctuation. III

LA 545 Show that you can use various forms and techniques to demonstrate skill in expository writing. III

LA 547 Show that you can prepare and present a written argument. III

Grammar SKILLS

PRIMARY

LA 110 Show your understanding of the elements of sentence structure. II

TERMINAL OBJECTIVES

LA 115 Show your understanding of common nouns, proper nouns, and pronouns in sentences. II

LA 120 Show that you can recognize and use correct verb forms in sentences. III

LA 125 Show that you can correctly apply the following: period, question mark, capital letters, and indentation. III

INTERMEDIATE

LA 265 Show that you can apply the transformational rules of grammar. III

LA 270 Show that you can apply the fundamental rules of grammar. III

LA 275 Show that you can apply the inflectional morphology rules of grammar. III

LA 280 Show that you can apply the derivational morphology rules of grammar. III

LA 285 Show that you can write sentences using the basic parts of speech correctly. III

LA 290 Show that you can write sentences using various types of sentence structure. III

LA 295 Show that you can apply rules of punctuation and capitalization. III

STUDY SKILLS

PRIMARY

LA 130 Show that you know about instructional materials in the classroom. I

LA 135 Show that you can use and care for materials and equipment. III

TERMINAL OBJECTIVES

LA 140 Show that you can use reference sources to locate and use information. III

INTERMEDIATE

LA 300 Show that you can select reading material suitable to your reading level. III

LA 305 Show that you can adjust your reading rate to the purpose and type of material. III

LA 310 Show that you can apply reading techniques to take notes. III

LA 315 Show that you can recognize and use all the parts of a book. III

LA 320 Show that you can use a dictionary to locate words and to identify their structure and meaning. III

LA 325 Show that you can find information in the library. III

LA 330 Show that you can use reference material to find information. III

LA 335 Show that you can find information for the purposes of summarizing, making generalizations, and identifying conclusions. III

LA 340 Show that you can prepare various types of outlines. III

LA 345 Demonstrate your ability to combine concepts, principles, and generalizations by producing a factual report from notes and an outline. V

SECONDARY

LA 550 Show your understanding of strategies for taking tests. II

LA 555 Show your understanding of strategies involved in developing good study skills. II

TERMINAL OBJECTIVES

LA 557 Make judgments based on the evaluation of dictionaries. VI

LA 560 Show that you can use the research skills and resources needed for a research paper. III

LA 565 Demonstrate your ability to perceive differences in written presentations by analyzing various documents. IV

LA 570 Demonstrate your ability to combine the necessary elements of research and organization by writing a research paper. IV

PERSONAL COMMUNICATION AND DEVELOPMENT SKILLS

PRIMARY

LA 145 Show that you can use the telephone. III

LA 150 Show that you can write friendly letters. III

INTERMEDIATE

LA 350 Show your understanding of appropriate and inappropriate forms of conversation. II

LA 355 Show that you can write friendly and business letters using the correct format. III

LA 360 Show that you can use skills of non-verbal communication. III

SECONDARY

LA 575 Show your understanding of military obligations. II

LA 580 Show that you can use information about various occupations, your interests, and your test scores to suggest first and second choices of long range goals. III

TERMINAL OBJECTIVES

LA 585 Show that you can use logic and rhetoric to solve problems, to write and discuss material, and to present arguments or debates. III

HISTORY AND DIALECTOLOGY

PRIMARY

LA 155 Show your understanding of language usage by recognizing varieties of expression.

INTERMEDIATE

LA 365 Show your understanding of Latin and Greek prefixes by deriving the meaning of words. II

LA 370 Show that you can trace the history of a linguistic form (word). III

LA 375 Show your understanding of regional differences in vocabulary, grammar, and punctuation. II

SECONDARY

LA 590 Show that you can find and use information about changes that have occurred in the development of language. III

LA 595 Demonstrate your ability to perceive relationships in theories of language development. IV

LA 600 Demonstrate your ability to perceive the relationship of emotional and psychological impact of words to semantics. IV

TERMINAL OBJECTIVES

CLASSIFICATION, INTERPRETATION, AND ANALYSIS OF LITERARY FORMS

PRIMARY

LA 160 Show your understanding of fact and fantasy in literature. II

LA 165 Show your understanding of a literary selection by reading with 75 percent to 90 percent comprehension. II

LA 170 Show your understanding of contextual clues. II

LA 175 Show that you can apply reading to personal experience. III

INTERMEDIATE

LA 380 Show your understanding of genre by classifying literary selections.

LA 385 Show your understanding of the main ideas and supporting ideas in literary selections. II

LA 390 Show your understanding of the personality traits of literary characters. II

LA 395 Show your understanding of literary selections by making inferences based on details. II

LA 400 Show your understanding of cause and effect relationships in literary selections. II

LA 405 Show your understanding of the setting in literary selections. II

LA 410 Show your understanding of plot development in literary selections. II

TERMINAL OBJECTIVES

LA 415 Demonstrate your ability to perceive the author's intent and/or point of view in literary selections. IV

LA 420 Demonstrate your ability to perceive mood and tone in literary selections. IV

LA 425 Make judgments involving the comparison of reading selections to personal experiences. VI

LA 430 Show your understanding of literary devices in given selections. II

SECONDARY

LA 605 Show your understanding of literary terms and devices by recognizing them in the short story, the novel, drama, biography, and poetry. II

LA 610 Make a judgment involving the evaluation of a preference for a literary genre. Use the characteristics of each genre as criteria for your selection. VI

LA 615 Demonstrate your ability to perceive relationships in the major works of an American poet. IV

LA 620 Demonstrate your ability to perceive the techniques that Shakespeare employed in comedy and tragedy, and then distinguish the major characteristics of both types of drama. IV

LA 625 Demonstrate your ability to perceive components and relationships in essays, using techniques of literary criticism. IV

LA 630 Demonstrate your ability to perceive components and relationships in short stories, using techniques of literary criticism. IV

LA 635 Demonstrate your ability to perceive components and relationships in novels, using techniques of literary criticism and interpretation. IV

TERMINAL OBJECTIVES

LA 640 Demonstrate your ability to perceive components and relationships in character motivation and action. IV

LA 645 Demonstrate your ability to perceive components and relationships in central conflicts between characters and/or ideas. IV

LA 650 Demonstrate your ability to combine concepts, principles, and generalizations by developing your own definition of culture and civilization based on literature that presents an anthropological view of man. V

LA 655 Demonstrate your ability to perceive the relationship of literary contributions of black writers to development of an understanding of the historical and contemporary problems of black Americans. IV

LA 660 Demonstrate your ability to perceive the relationship of intellectual and social implications in literature. IV

ORIGINAL WRITING

PRIMARY

LA 180 Show that you can use descriptive words or phrases. III

LA 185 Demonstrate your ability to combine concepts, principles, and generalizations by writing original stories. V

LA 190 Demonstrate your ability to combine concepts, principles, and generalizations by writing original poems. V

LA 195 Demonstrate your ability to combine concepts, principles, and generalizations by organizing factual information. V

INTERMEDIATE

LA 435 Show that you can use techniques of creative writing. III

TERMINAL OBJECTIVES

LA 440 Demonstrate your ability to combine concepts, principles, and generalizations by writing original compositions. V

SECONDARY

LA 665 Show your understanding of differences in style in written material. II

LA 670 Show that you can use dialogue to develop characterization. III

LA 675 Show that you can use special techniques in writing descriptively. III

LA 680 Using the techniques of creative writing, demonstrate your ability to combine concepts, principles, and generalizations by writing original compositions. V

Oral and Dramatic Interpretation

PRIMARY

LA 196 Show that you can dramatize ideas, emotions, and characters. III

INTERMEDIATE

LA 445 Demonstrate your ability to combine concepts, principles, and generalizations by developing dramatic techniques. V

LA 450 Show that you can make a variety of oral presentations. III

SECONDARY

LA 685 Show that you can present oral interpretations. III

TERMINAL OBJECTIVES

CRITICAL ANALYSIS OF MEDIA

INTERMEDIATE

LA 455 Show your understanding of the importance of mass media to individuals and to large populations. II

LA 460 Demonstrate your ability to perceive effects of television. IV

LA 465 Show that you can differentiate among statements of fact, fiction, and opinion. III

LA 470 Demonstrate your ability to perceive the techniques and effects of advertising. IV

LA 475 Demonstrate your ability to combine concepts, principles and generalizations by producing a simple newspaper (no less than one page) that includes one article of class (local) interest, one article of school (national) interest, one article of community (world) interest, and one article from each of the following sections: classified, sports, world news, theater-entertainment, editorial, and comics. V

SECONDARY

LA 690 Show that you can use techniques of mass media for persuading an audience. III

LA 695 Make judgments about media by evaluating different presentations. VI

INDEX

INDEX

INDEX

INDEX

INDEX

INDEX

INDEX

INDEX

INDEX

INDEX

INDEX

INDEX

INDEX

INDEX

INDEX

INDEX

INDEX

INDEX

INDEX

INDEX

INDEX

INDEX

INDEX

INDEX

INDEX

Behavioral Objectives

A Guide to Individualizing Learning

Text: Videocomp 9 point Roma with 10 point Roma Bold, display lines in 14 point Dimensia

Design and art: Steven Jacobs Design, Palo Alto, California

Editorial and production: Westinghouse Learning Press, Palo Alto, California

Composition, lithography, binding, packaging: Kingsport Press, Kingsport, Tennessee